Ghosts of Devon

Peter Underwood

President of The Ghost Club Society

Bossiney Books • Launceston

FOR
Deryck and Hazel Seymour
to whom ghosts are no strangers
with gratitude and affection

Illustration acknowledgements

Front cover by David C Golby

Drawings by Paul Honeywill

Original design by Penwell Ltd, Kelly Bray, Callington, Cornwall

Photograph(s) on pages 5, 7, 9, 11, 18, 29, 38, 43, 49, 51, 72, 95 and 98 by David C Golby; on pages 41, 44, 46, 47, 59, 61, 69, 72, 77, 80, 91, 104, 106 and 108 by Ray Bishop; on page 67 courtesy of Mrs B Dickinson; on pages 31 and 32 by Roy Westlake; on page 52 courtesy of Devon Library Services; on page 83 by John Chard; on page 6 by Chris Chapman; and on page 34 by Richard Isbell.

Published by Bossiney Books, Langore, Launceston, Cornwall PL15 8LD

First published in 1982

This reprint 2003

Copyright © 1982 Peter Underwood

ISBN 0-906456-62-2

Printed by R Booth Ltd, Mabe, Cornwall

About the Author

Peter Underwood FRSA is Life President of that famous investigating organisation, The Ghost Club Society, and he must have heard more first-hand ghost stories than any other person alive.

A long-standing member of The Society for Psychical Research, Vice-President of the Unitarian Society for Psychical Studies, a member of The Folklore Society, The Dracula Society and a former member of the Research Committee of the Psychic Research Organisation, he has lectured, written and broadcast extensively. He took part in the first official investigation into a haunting, and has sat with physical and mental mediums, and conducted investigations at seances. He has also been present at exorcisms and experiments with dowsing, precognition, clairvoyance, hypnotism and regression. He has conducted world-wide tests in telepathy and extra-sensory perception, and has personally investigated scores of haunted houses.

He possesses comprehensive files of alleged hauntings in every county of the British Isles as well as in many foreign countries, and his knowledge and experience have resulted in his being interviewed and consulted on psychic and occult matters by such organisations as the BBC and ITV.

Born at Letchworth Garden City in Hertfordshire, he now lives in a small village in Hampshire. He is a former Honorary Librarian of the London Savage Club, 1 Whitehall Place, London SW1A 2HD, where he can be contacted.

Other Bossiney Books by Peter Underwood

Ghosts of Cornwall

Travelling through this beautiful county of mystery and magic, Peter Underwood relates strange happenings that cannot easily be explained by known laws of nature.

Ghosts of Somerset

Somerset, according to Peter Underwood, is a rich hunting ground for the ghost enthusiast. Throughout its million acres there are scores of places, including Sedgemoor, Bath, Dunster and Glastonbury, that have individual ghostly associations.

Ghosts of North Devon

The author relates inexplicable happenings told to him personally by both holiday makers and people living locally in North Devon. This attractive countryside it seems, with its thatched cottages, sandy beaches and twisting leafy lanes, belies a deeper mystery of magic and the supernatural.

Ghostly Encounters in the South-west

Britain's number one ghost hunter explores ghostly encounters in Cornwall, Devon and Somerset – the bizarre goings-on in a farmhouse on the Cornish moors, the supernatural happenings in an Exeter hospital, and a phantom hitch-hiker in Somerset are just three examples.

West Country Hauntings

According to the author, the West Country offers 'just about every kind of ghostly manifestation under the sun'. In this book he investigates a goodly number at some of the most haunted places in Devon, Cornwall and Somerset.

'Devon is a land full of mystery and
of ghostly lore and legend.'

Introduction

The ghosts of Devon are to be found in such great centres as Torquay, Exeter and Ilfracombe, along the glorious coastline, and in the hinterland with its moors and hamlets, tall grey churches, green leafy tunnels and lush lanes. Wherever you go in Devon you will find stories of ghosts and ghostly happenings, fascinating accounts of paranormal experiences that defy complete explanation even in these days of scepticism and scientific wonders.

If I can whet the appetite with these true stories of haunted inns

'Wherever you go in Devon you will find stories of ghosts and ghostly happenings.'

and churches, of ghostly manors and halls, of spectral monks and phantom footsteps, of sounds and shapes and entities that are as remarkable as they are bewildering, then I will be satisfied. If I can only get you to explore Devon then perhaps you will experience some of the individual and indeed unique ghosts and legends that saturate this lovely county.

Devon, glorious Devon, is a land full of mystery and of ghostly lore and legend; a land where it seems there is a subtle link between this world and the next; where centuries do not matter and time, occasionally, stands still. For the enquiring mind the countryside, the people and the ghosts of Devon have an inexhaustible attraction.

My selection is representative and for every ghost and haunting I have included there is another and another . . . perhaps you know one true ghost story that might be included in a future volume?

The Savage Club   Peter Underwood
Fitzmaurice Place
Berkeley Square
London W 1

**'If I can whet the appetite with these true stories
of haunted inns and churches, spectral monks and
phantom footsteps . . .' ▶**

GHOSTS
of Devon

Abbotskerswell

A few years ago there was considerable publicity here following the frightening experiences of a young married couple, John and Carol Durston. It was only a few weeks after they were married and had moved into the ground-floor flat of 200-year old Aller House. For ten days they were happy and had just about settled in when they both saw the ghost.

First they heard footsteps at night and a curious shuffling noise. They had been asleep for an hour or so when they both found themselves wide awake and listening to the sound of heavy footsteps in the corridor outside their flat. They heard a lot of shuffling too and movement that sounded like someone walking up and down the corridor and then eventually the footsteps faded as they sounded on the stairs. The young couple decided that someone must have come in late and they turned over and resumed their sleep.

The next evening they were just thinking about going to bed when they heard the noises again: distinct and heavy footsteps and the sound of shuffling. John went out to see what was going on. Once he was in the corridor outside their flat he could still hear the footsteps and they seemed to be all around him and quite close but he saw nothing.

The following evening, a chilly one for September, the young couple built a big fire, settled down and enjoyed an evening of television. As they switched off the set the room suddenly went stone cold although a good fire was still burning. They were both

'Devon is a land where it seems there is a subtle link between ▶
this world and the next . . .'

shivering as they went to bed but they spent an undisturbed night.

The next night the real terror began. They were in bed when they heard the footsteps again and then a single 'clink' from the direction of the mantelpiece in the room they were occupying. John switched on the light and Carol immediately noticed that a tiny ornamental donkey had been moved to the end of the mantelpiece from its usual position in the centre.

She jumped out of bed and replaced it in the middle of the mantelpiece beside a large sea shell, and returned to bed and tried to go back to sleep. As soon as the light was switched off there was another 'clinking' sound. They jumped up, switched on the light, and found that the donkey had been moved again! After that the movement of the donkey and the shell became almost a nightly routine and always, just before any noise or movement of an object, they noticed that the room became icy cold although they were careful to ensure that a good fire blazed in the hearth.

A few days later Carol was preparing a meal in the kitchen and John was reading in the next room. John described the first sighting of the ghost: 'I noticed that the room suddenly felt icy cold and then I heard a noise from the direction of the window and when I looked I saw a whitish cloud of mist, shaped like a fat man. I found that I was paralysed and couldn't say a word. As I watched the mist evaporated and the room became warm again.'

Just then Carol came into the room and the smile on her face froze as she looked at her husband. 'John,' she called. 'What is it — you look as though you have seen a ghost!' John didn't look up as he huskily replied, 'I have . . .'

Carol said afterwards that at this stage she still didn't believe in ghosts but from that moment she felt uneasy and somehow insecure in the flat during the daytime whenever John was out. Then one night she saw the same figure. 'It was horrifying . . . but we didn't tell anyone, we thought they would only laugh at us.' Meanwhile the ghostly happenings became more noisy and more violent. Once they were sitting on the settee, one at either end, when the room became suddenly cold and they both saw the misty form of a fat man sitting between them.

' . . . the room became suddenly cold and they both saw the misty form of a fat man sitting between them.' ▶

Another evening, after the room had suddenly become freezing cold, the lampshade began to spin round and round, faster and faster, until the wire, curling up, forced it to stop and spin the other way. John took hold of it and began to unwind the wire but before he had time to complete the second round, it suddenly stopped for an instant and then spun back again. This 'game' continued for about ten minutes. 'I was determined not to give in,' said John. 'But the ghost had more patience and he won.' Eventually, left to itself, the lamp stopped winding and unwinding and the room gradually resumed its normal temperature.

That night the noises of footsteps and shuffling became even louder and, as the terrified couple clung to each other wondering what was going to happen next, the white mist appeared in the room and 'walked' up and down. From then onwards it was seen in the room at night. Sometimes it opened doors; at other times it seemed to appear and disappear through some panelling. Once it shook a heavy bedroom cupboard as though it were a baby's rattle. When this was happening John switched on the light and they both saw the cupboard moving. Then the ghost started to roll up the edge of the carpet.

By this time John and Carol had had enough. Although it was two o'clock in the morning, they got up and dressed as fast as they could and walked two miles to the home of John's mother where they spent the rest of the night.

They tried to move back into the flat several times but things were so bad that they couldn't bear it for more than a few hours although, because of the difficulty they had had in obtaining the flat in the first place and the problem of finding another, they didn't want to leave altogether. In desperation they went to see the Reverend Gordon Langford, vicar of Abbotskerswell.

'I didn't laugh at what they told me,' the vicar said at the time. 'Instead I listened sympathetically and then went to the flat with them. I neither saw nor felt anything extraordinary, but then I am not in the least sensitive to that sort of manifestation . . . John seems to be a healthy, sensible sort of fellow and Carol seems perfectly normal and down-to-earth, not at all a neurotic type, so I decided to do a little investigation for myself.'

He discovered that there was once a factory behind the house and that the young couple's flat was once used as an office for the factory. In 1925, at a time when the firm's books were being audited, a man named Victor Judd had committed suicide. After the factory was pulled down in 1939 the tenants of the house were frequently troubled by mysterious noises.

One tenant, an elderly lady, said she had noticed nothing unusual while she was there but her two dogs certainly did. Eventually she was forced to move because they kept howling in terror night after night.

Some years later the house was put up for sale and a professional man and his wife and his father, a business man, all very practical and realistic people, went to view the house. They spent about five minutes in the place and they left because they all felt instinctively that the house was haunted. They told the estate agent they had all 'felt a presence there'.

The vicar also discovered that local people remembered an incident years earlier when a man had hanged himself beside a window in the flat where John and Carol had lived and he learned that after the young couple left their flat, other tenants in the building reported that they had continually heard the sound of heavy footsteps, apparently emanating from the couple's empty room. These witnesses included Mr Leonard Culley, who lived in the other ground-floor flat with his family, and he and his wife had often been woken up at night by the noises coming from the empty Durston flat.

The Reverend Gordon Langford reported the matter to the Bishop of Exeter, Dr Robert Mortimer, and he sent one of his chaplains, the Reverend Sir Patrick Ferguson-Davie to investigate. At the flat, sitting near the fireplace, Sir Patrick said, 'I know there is a ghost here. I am stone cold from toe to waist.' Following this preliminary visit the Bishop visited the house, sprinkling holy water and conducting a thirty-five minute service of exorcism. Carol and John were present and Carol said afterwards: 'During the service the ghost stood right behind us. It made a lot of noise as if it was fighting against the exorcism, but halfway through it gave in and disappeared. We have had no trouble since.'

However a month later Mr and Mrs Culley believed that the ghost had moved into their flat across the passage and it seemed that the Bishop's exorcism had had little effect on the ghost. The Culleys arranged for four mediums to visit the house after claiming to see the ghost in the kitchen of their flat. Mrs Culley said a kind of mist appeared in front of an airing cupboard and then she saw a shadowy figure.

I am indebted to my friend Dr Peter Hilton-Rowe for information on this fascinating case and the last I heard about it was a letter from Peter's brother, the Reverend Alan Rowe who, writing a month after the Culley's experience, says he saw Carol Durston a few days earlier and she said, 'Our friend has come back to the flat!' According to what she told the vicar of Kingskerswell, she and her husband went into the room one evening and found it icy cold and then they saw the misty figure sitting in a chair. It rose and moved past them and out of the room. Perhaps understandably the couple decided to definitely leave Aller House.

Aveton Gifford

According to the *Transactions of the Devonshire Association* (35th Report on Folklore, 1935) there are, or were, three ghosts at South Efford House.

The house was occupied many years ago by a naval officer who for some long forgotten reason seems to have positively hated the inhabitants of this estuary village where the ancient church of singular beauty was almost totally destroyed in a World War II air raid. In life the officer would often be seen leaning out of a window berating courting couples who passed by or indeed anyone within earshot, and he reportedly died still vehemently and loudly cursing the villagers. It is claimed that he still does so in death.

The second ghost is that of a manservant who hanged himself from an oak beam over one of the stairways and his ghost was long reputed to be seen where the tragedy took place, his slowly swinging body with bloated face frightening many a servant and visitor, before it slowly disappeared or rather dissolved into nothingness.

Finally there is the daytime ghost of a ferryman. He is said to have died of grief when the steps from the house to the river were moved by the owner who had the door opening onto them blocked up to prevent accidents. The ferryman's ghost was usually seen

'. . . his ghost was long reputed to be seen, his slowly swinging body frightening many a visitor.' ▶

carrying what looked like a crowbar with which, it is presumed, he planned to open the blocked-up door. It is reported that a massive cupboard, rising to within an inch of the ceiling, was found inexplicably moved eighteen inches from the wall where the old door to the ferry used to be and for years the owners of South Efford House could never persuade servants from the village to sleep in the house.

Berry Pomeroy

The haunted ruins of Berry Pomeroy Castle are isolated and hidden and full of atmosphere. They are approached by means of a long and winding leafy lane and the gaunt ruins stand starkly on a spur of land overlooking a brook.

If you are fortunate enough to visit Berry Pomeroy when it is deserted, or almost deserted, wander slowly through the ruins and over

Berry Pomeroy Castle: ' . . . you are more than likely to see or hear something of the ghosts associated with this place.'

the grass where once stood the great mansion within the ruins of what used to be a moated stronghold. Sit quietly by all means but keep fully alert and let your eyes wander time and again over and round these silent walls and you are more than likely to see or hear something of the ghosts that have been associated with this place for many years. If you have a camera with you, take lots of pictures for strange forms and shapes and odd effects have been repeatedly captured here on film. In 1968 the ghost of a man in a tricorn hat and another of a young woman in dark clothes were caught on photographs, near the entrance to St Margaret's Tower.

These lofty, ruined walls were once part of the proud mansion of the Seymours and before that the draughty castle of the Pomeroys who came to England with the Conqueror. Romance and mystery are thick in the air here and several ghosts have been seen and heard over the years.

The ancient Tower and the deep dungeons below harbour the ghost of Margaret, a Pomeroy, who was incarcerated here by her sister Eleanor. The far more beautiful Margaret had fallen in love with the same man as had her sister. Eleanor, at that time mistress of the castle, solved the problem by having Margaret forced down the circular steps and into the deep pit of the dungeon where she eventually died of starvation; but even now she cannot leave the ruins, it would seem, for the walls of the dungeons echo the tears and cries of despair and her ghostly form haunts the ramparts where she walks towards the tiny doorway that leads into the great guardroom over the gateway. If you wait quietly in the alcoves of the stone corridor you may see her, as not a few visitors have done.

Five hundred years after Eleanor and Margaret Pomeroy were here Sir Walter Farquhar, later to become a famous surgeon, visited the Seymour mansion, a building that had been badly damaged in a fire late in the seventeenth century. The Seymours left Pomeroy with a steward installed to look after the place. Young Dr Farquhar received a call to attend the wife of the steward; he went and walked into the greatest mystery of his life.

As he stood in an oak-panelled room with an enormous fireplace and a staircase in one corner, he saw a young girl enter the room; she was richly dressed and the doctor, thinking she had come to take him to his patient, moved towards her. She, however, completely ignored him and, seemingly in some distress, hurriedly crossed the room and mounted the stone stairway. As she did so she turned and

Dr Farquhar clearly saw her features. 'If ever a human face exhibited agony and remorse,' he said afterwards, 'those features were then presented to me . . .'

The ghost the doctor saw, for such she was, was a former daughter of one of the Pomeroys who is said to have been strangled in the room at the top of the stone stairway. It was only during a later visit, when the doctor chanced to mention the girl he had seen previously, that he was told the story of the ghost of the murdered girl and the fact that her apparition usually heralded a death . . . the steward's lady died soon afterwards. This ghost, a young girlish figure in rich apparel, has been glimpsed among the ruins at Berry Pomeroy in recent years and her wistful look lures those who see her to follow — but those who do follow the pathetic, silent figure, often find themselves in an unsafe spot and sometimes they have an accident.

There are stories too of the ghost of Margaret — or would it be Eleanor?— haunting the remains of St Margaret's Tower and luring the unwary to the deep and dark dungeons or elsewhere where an accident is likely . . . so if you should visit Berry Pomeroy and see a girlish figure, in the best tradition of the hardened ghost-hunter, stop where you are and watch and listen and note every detail of the experience . . . but do not follow, even if the figure beckons . . .

My friend James Turner was among the many visitors to Berry Pomeroy who, suddenly and quite inexplicably, had the overwhelming impression that the empty stone window frames contained real glass windows as they had long years ago. Even the sun seems to be reflected from these hollow mullioned windows on occasions and sometimes the sound of a baby crying or the faint sound of music played on strings is to be heard in this desolate place.

In particular an overwhelming and frightening feeling of isolation and evil has repeatedly been reported by visitors in the vicinity of some of the archways. Here too the figure of a woman dressed in a long, blue cape with a hood has been seen. So there are several things to remember when you visit haunted Berry Pomeroy: don't follow any figure you may see; be as quiet as possible and listen in

'. . . she cannot leave the ruins . . . her ghostly form haunts the ramparts . . .'▶

different parts of the ruins, and always have a camera ready to take a photograph or two.

A recent correspondent tells me that she and her family visited Berry Pomeroy on a sunny summer morning but they found the atmosphere unfriendly and they were glad to get away. They noticed immediately the unusual quiet of the place and the somehow stifling atmosphere and the fact that although there were trees all round, they heard no birds singing.

She and her sister, Helen, looked round the ruins and reached a tower and decided to descend its steps. 'The steps were very damp and Helen almost fell but I managed to grab her just in time, saving her from a nasty fall. When we reached the bottom it was icy cold and I didn't like it at all. I felt as though something unpleasant was going to happen to us and then Helen spoke my thoughts: "Let's go, I don't like it here", and we scrabbled up into daylight. We all felt the place was really evil. It was only later when we read a guide book that we learned that the tower Helen and I went into was known as St Margaret's Tower and that it was reputedly haunted by a ghost who lured people to their deaths by falling into the depths of the tower.'

Bideford

An old house here, on the outskirts of the town, used to be the home of William and Maria Done, the grandparents of Carol Done whom I met through my old friend Alisdair Alpin MacGregor. Eventually Carol's grandparents left the house in order, as they readily admitted, to get away from the ghosts.

At that time the large and rambling house, parts of which dated back to the early eighteenth century, stood among thick woodland on a hillside overlooking the sea. It had a big garden laid out with flower beds and lawns and shrubberies: a garden that was undoubtedly haunted.

One bright summer morning Carol was sitting on the trunk of a fallen tree, at the top of the garden, when she chanced to glance up. She was thinking how lovely and peaceful it all was when she was surprised to see a little old lady in crinoline and sunbonnet, standing at the far edge of the lawn, seemingly peering intently at the flower border at her feet.

Although she could not see the face of the figure which had its back to her, Carol had the vivid impression of tranquillity and friendliness, epitomising, as she used to say, the atmosphere of the old house and garden.

Carol watched the figure for a minute or two and then the form disappeared from sight behind a shrub. The quiet presence of the little old lady fitted so well into the background of the place that Carol took her existence for granted and in some strange way she accepted the presence of the unknown intruder to such an extent that she did not mention to anyone what she had seen.

Years later, after her grandparents had left the house, she did chance to mention the matter to her mother who was immediately most interested, telling her daughter that a ghostly old lady, such as she had seen, had been observed in the garden many times by neighbours and visitors to the house, but the matter was never talked about. Usually she was seen wandering wistfully among the roses on sunny mornings.

One day in 1938, four years after her grandparents were dead, Carol suggested to her mother and father that it would be nice to re-visit the old house where her grandparents had lived and where she had spent so many happy holidays. They made enquiries and discovered that the house was again empty. They obtained the keys from an estate agent who told them that nobody seemed to stay in the house very long.

Arriving at the house they walked together up the drive, becoming more and more depressed at the appearance of the overgrown and neglected garden and, inside the house, the empty rooms and feeling of despair and rejection that seemed to hang heavily over the place. As they passed, almost in silence, from room to room, they each separately became aware of an uncanny aura brooding over everything. They saw no ghost on this visit and were not surprised for they felt, quite rightly, that the house needed to be inhabited to be haunted.

Another ghost was occasionally seen both inside the house and in the garden and especially on the drive and pathway leading to the house. This form, an elderly man, had been identified and was referred to for years as 'Old Sam', a former family retainer. He was often seen by the Done family and sometimes by visitors: a tall, stooping figure, most often walking up the drive towards the house.

This ghost also frequented the vicinity of the gardener's cottage which was situated at the steep bend in the drive connecting the property with the road to Bideford and there was a garage adjoining. This garage, a converted stable, had a glass roof enabling one to look down into it from two of the cottage windows.

Not infrequently, and usually late at night, the gardener and his wife, Mr and Mrs William Butler, would notice a dim and mysterious light in the garage below. At first they thought a tramp had entered the property but whenever William Butler crept quietly down and stealthily investigated, he found the door of the garage securely locked. Eventually both he and his wife became so accustomed to seeing this inexplicable light that they paid little or no attention to it.

One morning, soon after the gardener had left the cottage to attend to his duties, Mrs Butler heard a knock at the door. Not expecting a visitor so early in the day, she hurried upstairs to tidy herself before answering the door. As she turned to go back downstairs the knock was repeated and a moment later she opened the door in time to see the tall, stooping figure of a man retreating down the garden path. It was 'Old Sam' and she was understandably mildly surprised. 'If I had answered the first knock,' she told her husband, 'I must have found him on the doorstep — and that might have been too much for me . . .'

A few days later Helen Done, Carol's mother, was doing some ironing in the kitchen of the old house when she happened to look out of the window. In so doing she noticed 'Old Sam' strolling along the terrace towards the front door. Hastily putting down the iron, she hurried to the door, confident that on opening it she would at last meet the phantom face to face, but by the time she opened the door, there was no trace of 'Old Sam'.

The visitations of 'Old Sam' and to a lesser degree, of the little old lady in the garden, well-meaning and harmless as they may have been, became so frequent and disturbing to the occupants and their servants and sometimes to visitors, that the Done family sold the house and moved. A later occupant found the sudden appearance of the ghosts so unbearable that he tried to hang himself. As Carol

◄ **The Author, President of The Ghost Club, has probably heard more first-hand ghost stories than any man alive.**

used to say: 'A friendly and occasional ghost is one thing; a persistent ghostly caller is quite another!'

Bridestowe

Strange disturbances of varying intensity have been reported over the years at Great Bidlake, an attractive Elizabethan manor house with later additions: a property where, it has long been thought, a murder took place at the time of the Civil Wars.

At that time the house was occupied by Squire Bidlake, a good Royalist, who fled for his life one day when he received word that Roundhead troops were approaching the house: indeed as he hurriedly set off he was alarmed to see a party of Roundheads coming towards him along the drive. It was too late for him to run for they had already seen him and he quickly decided to walk boldly through them, hoping they would not recognize him. When they asked him whether Squire Bidlake was at the house, he artfully replied, 'He was when I left' and hastened on his way. As soon as he was out of sight he hid himself in a tree and remained there until the search was over and the troops had left.

In view of subsequent experiences over the years one is inclined to wonder whether something of the all-embracing, blood-chilling and overwhelming physical fear that the Squire must have experienced on that occasion, has in some way that we do not yet understand, lingered here and been sensed on occasions by people centuries later.

Miss E. Cornish told my friend, Deryck Seymour, that one bright summer afternoon she and a friend were walking down the long drive towards the house when Miss Cornish was suddenly aware of a feeling of great fear, imminent danger, almost physical illness. By the time they reached the house the feeling was so intense that she felt ready to run for her life. Glancing at her friend, she was surprised to see that she too was obviously agitated and in fact looked truly ill. By mutual consent they hurriedly retraced their steps. Once clear of the drive they recovered. Neither, at the time of this experience, knew that Great Bidlake was reputed to be haunted.

On 10 April 1956, Deryck Seymour found himself in the vicinity and decided to call at Great Bidlake. He came across a girl halfway up the drive who told him she was employed there. When he asked whether it might be possible for him to see something of the house, she immediately offered to take him to see her master. On enquiring whether she lived in, she replied that she always went home at night and she would never dream of sleeping there. She said the house was well-known to be haunted but she had no fear of it by day.

Deryck Seymour met the then owner's son who readily showed his visitor round the house and discussed the alleged haunting. He said that every so often all the occupants would pass a restless night, continuously being disturbed by knockings and heavy footsteps and the opening and closing of doors, for which no rational explanation was ever found. Only his grandmother had ever *seen* anything, he went on. Once she had awakened in her room and distinctly seen a female form, which at first she took to be the maid with her early morning cup of tea. She asked the girl to put the tea down — whereupon the figure vanished and looking at her bedside clock the old lady saw that it was 2 o'clock in the morning.

After a night of disturbances, Deryck Seymour was told, all might be calm for several weeks. Perhaps these weeks have now extended into months or even years for the present occupant, Mr B.G. Birkmyre, informed me in October 1981 that he had never heard of any story of a resident ghost but he was kind enough to tell me one or two snippets of interest. He says there have been 'repeated occurrences of a voice, calling a name or laughing, sounding like a young girl'; their housekeeper and her husband have both 'heard the sound of a baby crying in their bedroom' and, he adds, 'I, the most unlikely sort of person for this sort of thing, saw a woman cross the hall towards the kitchen; this in broad daylight of a summer evening and myself completely sober! All somewhat mysterious, but apparently without particular relevance.' And, I was told quite recently, people still occasionally report inexplicable knockings, taps and bangs, the sound of doors opening and closing and then there are the eternal footsteps, the commonest of all reported sounds in houses that have been haunted in the past and still may be.

Brixham

When I was compiling the first-ever comprehensive gazetteer of British ghosts (published in 1971 and reprinted in 1975) I visited the ancient and ominously-named Black House at Higher Brixham; a property so old that it was used by the monks when they were building the fourteenth-century church of St Mary's on the opposite side of the road. It is a fascinating building, full of odd corners, unexpected passages and rooms; it even has an *art noveau* stained glass door.

The house has long had the reputation of being haunted and until quite recently local people were reluctant to pass the place at night. Rooms would light up unaccountably, strange noises would be heard and the inexplicable figure of a man would be seen at one of the windows of this rabbit-warren of a house.

During World War II Miss Evelyn Joyce lived at the Black House with her father and a housekeeper. One winter evening, as they came into the house, there was a knock at the front door. There they found the local police constable who told them that the light in the room over the porch was contravening the black-out regulations. The police officer was invited into the house and assured that there was no one else in the house at that time and that there was no light in any upstairs window. Investigation showed that sure enough there was no light by that time but the policeman stuck to his story and described in some detail the contents of the room and the figure of an old man he had seen plainly from the road outside; a man in strange, out-of-date clothes.

Miss Joyce told me that doors in the house often locked by themselves and on occasions she had found herself locked inside various rooms. Once a carpenter had to saw through locks and bolts to release her. Several times she had found herself locked outside the house, too.

Miss Joyce related to my wife and me a long list of unexplained noises; loud cracks and bangs, rhythmic and prolonged, followed by complete silence; a moaning or sighing sound that seemed to coincide with a full moon; the clatter of horses' hooves, seemingly on cobble stones but emanating from a lawn where once there had been a stable yard; and footsteps, sometimes stealthy and quick and at other times heavy and loud, that have been heard from many parts of the house but particularly in the vicinity of the carved staircase.

Black House, Brixham: '. . . the inexplicable figure of a man would be seen at one of the windows . . .'▶

There is a story that in the fifteenth century the property was occupied by one Squire Hilliard whose son fell in love with a country girl from Churston but his father arranged for the girl to marry some-one else. The son saw his beloved coming out of the church on the arm of another man and promptly hanged himself, leaving his horse to find its way home riderless. Now the ghost of Squire Hilliard locks doors to keep his angry son away and also searches for his son to seek forgiveness and the ghostly clatter of horses' hooves recall that fearful day.

Buckland Abbey

Buckland Abbey, the home of Sir Francis Drake, teems with re-ported ghosts and strange legends. Even the extensions he made to this Cistercian Abbey built in 1278 were, it is said, completed in only three nights with the help of the devil. So successful was Drake with his victory over the Armada and other achievements against overwhelming and seemingly impossible odds that the belief grew —both during his lifetime and after his death—that he must have allied himself with the devil and had perhaps sold his soul in return for the invincible powers of seamanship and warfare that he undoubtedly possessed.

In particular it was widely believed that the pact was made at the place now known as Devil's Point in exchange for the storm that drove the Spanish fleet northwards to its doom. Devil's Point is reported to be haunted to this day by the ghosts of magicians and witches who took part in the satanic ceremony; many people have reported hearing and seeing strange figures muttering their mysterious incantations.

Such an unholy alliance, whispered his countrymen, was why he and his friend Sir Richard Grenville had no compunction in turning a Cistercian establishment into a domestic residence. Can it be that the imps and demons that were his servants during his lifetime still

Drake, it was believed, made a pact with the devil in exchange for the storm that drove the Spanish Armada northwards to its doom.▶

hold sway over his soul and give him no peace?

Drake's famous drum, preserved here, accompanied the Admiral when he circumnavigated the globe in 1577-80. For four centuries it has been said that Drake is not dead but sleeping, and if his drum is beaten in times of peril for the country, he will awake and emerge from Buckland Abbey and once again use his magical powers to save his beloved England.

There is a story that as he lay dying of dysentry in 1596, on board a ship in Nombre de Dios bay, he signified that his drum was to be taken to Buckland Abbey and he intimated that if England was ever again in serious danger and the drum was beaten, he could hear its note and return from beyond the grave to aid his country. The story was immortalized in Newbolt's poem.

Gradually the legend of Drake's drum has changed and for years now it has been believed that the drum is heard, beating by itself,

If Drake's drum, preserved at Buckland Abbey, below, is beaten in times of peril, he will awake and once again use his magical powers to save his beloved England.

when the country is in danger. It is supposed to have been heard in 1914 before the outbreak of the Great War; again (somewhat puzzlingly) either in 1918 when the German fleet was completely surrounded and surrendered or in 1919 when the German fleet was scuttled in Scapa Flow; and in 1939 before the Second World War — this time in the vicinity of Combe Sydenham House where Drake lived after his marriage to Elizabeth Sydenham in 1585.

That marriage has a legend of its own. Elizabeth's noble family at first refused to permit the match for they were aware of Drake's humble origin — his parentage and even the exact date of his birth being doubtful — and Drake went back to sea. At length Elizabeth became tired of waiting for him and she became betrothed to a man of her parents' choice.

On the wedding day, as the bridal party approached the door of Stogumber Church, there was a blinding flash and a thunderous roar in the sky. A huge cannonball fell at the feet of the bride who was convinced that Drake had somehow known of her impending marriage and had fired a shot across the world to show his anger. She refused to allow the ceremony to continue and in due course Drake returned and the couple were married. A meteorite, nearly as big as a football, was preserved in the hall at Combe Sydenham House and this was said to be the mysterious 'cannonball'.

And still on moonless, stormy nights, Sir Francis Drake, perhaps the most famous of all Devon ghosts, is said to sometimes be seen to this day, seated in a coach, lashing a team of headless horses into a wild gallop out of Buckland Abbey and across Dartmoor . . .

Chagford

The Three Crowns Hotel was described by Charles Kingsley as 'a beautiful old mullioned and gabled perpendicular inn'. It was built of Dartmoor granite in the thirteenth century and the old-world atmosphere is still evident from the great fireplace and the massive oaken beams. On one of the stone seats in the unusual porch a young Cavalier and poet, Sydney Godolphin, died after a skirmish with the Roundheads in 1642. He has been described as 'one of the four wheels of Charles' wain' and his portrait hangs in the Godolphin lounge.

The gentle ghost of Sydney Godolphin has been seen and heard in this comfortable one-time manor house. A Ghost Club member saw the figure of a Cavalier pass along a corridor one night and disappear into a wall; next morning he recognized the ghost from the portrait. Other visitors have reported hearing heavy footsteps, as of a booted man, passing through their rooms with nothing visible to account for the sounds.

Some years ago the photographer and publisher, Mr M.G. Hamilton-Fisher, told me that proprietors past and present had some weird and wonderful ghost tales to tell about poor old Sydney Godolphin. When Mr Hamilton-Fisher was taking photographs for the hotel's brochure he even had trouble taking the interior photograph of the Godolphin lounge until he included the Sydney Godolphin portrait in the picture. Then all went swimmingly. 'He is apparently rather a conceited spirit,' Mr Hamilton-Fisher told me,

The Three Crowns, Chagford: 'The gentle ghost of Sydney Godolphin, who died in the porch, has been seen and heard in this comfortable one-time manor house.'

'but quite harmless.'

Whiddon Park is a fine old house of granite, with mullioned windows and attractive chimneys, standing in deep seclusion a mile or so from Chagford. Here Mrs Duxbury, the wife of the late vicar of Bovey Tracey, lived before her marriage and she related to my friend Deryck Seymour some of the ghostly happenings that she had experienced.

When she first moved into the house with her family, she and her mother spent the first night in rooms with a connecting door which they took care to leave open. Her mother was expecting her husband to arrive very late that night and when both mother and daughter had long been in their beds they both heard the sounds of the front door opening and closing and of a man's footsteps mounting the stairs. The sounds seemed to come right up to the bedroom door and then they stopped. The mother called out, 'Is that you?' But there was no reply and thoroughly alarmed they both got out of their respective beds and eventually summoned up sufficient courage to open the bedroom door and go out onto the landing. Heartened at finding no one there but puzzled as to the cause of the footsteps they searched the whole house and found it completely deserted.

On another occasion Mrs Duxbury was alone in the house expecting a painter and decorator to call. She was upstairs when she heard heavy footsteps on the stairs and she called out, 'Come along up . . .' But once again all was quiet and there was no one in the house.

Another puzzling incident which occurred on three successive days after dark was a rapping on one of the downstairs windows. This disturbance had been heard before and was said to be caused by the ghost of a sailor but details of any story that may have given rise to the haunting have been lost. In any event no logical explanation was ever found for the rappings.

In August 1971 the daughter of the house was married at Chagford Church. On the morning of the wedding a guest at Whiddon Park found himself wide awake in the half light of dawn and he saw the form of a young woman in an old-fashioned wedding dress standing in the doorway. When he related this experience next morning he was told that the incident in *Lorna Doone* of the bride being shot at her wedding service was founded on fact for in the seventeenth century a bride from Whiddon Park was actually shot and killed at Chagford Church by a jealous lover. She was buried in

the churchyard there and her grave is known to this day.

After her wedding in 1971, as reported in the *Western Morning News* 14 August 1971, the bride placed her bouquet on the grave of the murdered bride. It is to be hoped that such a charming gesture placated for all time one of the ghosts that haunted Whiddon Park.

Colyton

This interesting and attractive little town is famous for its lace, its slate quarries that have provided material for so many billiard tables and its church with traces of Saxon masonry at the base of the tower and the notable tomb of the wife of the fifth Earl of Devon. It is also justly proud of its diverse hauntings: the ghost of a former vicar, a water spirit, a ghost cat and a haunted vicarage.

Early in the nineteenth century the Reverend Dr Frederick Barnes was chaplain to the House of Commons and vicar of Colyton. He loved the wonderful view of the surrounding country-side from the Hilltop and he took an old tombstone from the churchyard and had it positioned at his favourite spot so that he could sit and enjoy a pipe and take in the view that had been des-cribed as one of the finest in the whole of England. 'The Doctor's Stone' was there for many years and there are persistent stories that the ghost of Dr Barnes haunts the spot; usually he is seen sit-ting and resting, as he did so often in life, smoking his pipe and en-joying the peaceful scene spread out before him. Some witnesses say they have smelt tobacco smoke but have seen nothing; others have distinctly seen the figure of the reverend doctor from a distance but when they have approached the haunted place, it has been found to be deserted.

Legend has it that Katherine of Aragon stayed at the vicarage and for years a pomegranate tree in the garden was referred to as 'Katherine of Aragon's Tree'. Such a visit is not as unlikely as it may seem for Thomas Brerewode, who built the original structure, was a staunch supporter of Katherine when Henry VIII was ob-

◄'. . . a bride from Whiddon Park was actually shot
and killed at Chagford Church by a jealous lover.'

taining his divorce of convenience and there is a stone carved pomegranate, her emblem, outside the house, together with a Tudor Rose, the King's emblem. It must seem likely that Katherine was indeed here at a troubled period of her life, perhaps dreaming of the peace and quiet that might have been . . .

At all events the ghosts of Colyton Vicarage are quiet and peaceful. There is the ghost of Brerewode himself, thought to be worried about some valuables left in his keeping; there is the shade of Bishop Veysey, Bishop of Exeter (another of the Queen's supporters), noiselessly gliding through these ancient rooms and passages, still brooding perhaps on the troubles and perplexities of the world while at other times his footsteps are heard and a gentle dragging sound, as of vestments trailing along the floor; sometimes again there is merely an overwhelming impression of the

Colyton Vicarage: ' . . . the ghost of an Elizabethan lady has been seen walking pensively in the garden.'

presence of 'something', but something pleasant, the presence of a good and kindly person. And then there is the ghost of an Elizabethan lady—Katherine herself perhaps?—that has been seen on quiet summer evenings, walking pensively in the garden.

There is a haunted field at Colyton. The local people call it 'Pan's Field' and occasionally, on still summer days, whispering voices have been heard from the vicinity of the stream that runs through the meadow. Ghosts often seem to be attracted to water and perhaps it would be possible to help this earth-bound water spirit if only the words could be distinguished but the whispering, distinct but without any words being recognisable, continues to be heard on rare occasions as it has been for centuries.

There is also an old house with a grey lady ghost, according to Mary Collier, a friendly phantom that is sometimes accompanied by a ghost cat. The occupants are used to being asked by visitors, 'Who is the lady in grey?' Sometimes she is seen sitting on one of the chairs and sometimes passing out of the room as humans enter it. Here too there is a ghost boy of perhaps ten or twelve who appears to date from the 1920s. He wears short trousers and an open-neck shirt. Once he appeared suddenly at the front door and as suddenly disappeared. He is probably a previous occupant of the house, like the mysterious lady who is sometimes seen in the garden. From her dress and hair she too would seem to date from some sixty years ago. But the present occupants say all the ghosts are friendly and they are never worried by their visitors from the past.

Coombe Cellars near Teignmouth

The Old Smuggler's Inn has long had the reputation of being haunted. In 1968 a barmaid at the old riverside public-house refused to sleep at the inn. She said her bedroom was haunted by the ghost of a woman who was murdered there and a legend exists that tells of a London lady visiting the inn in the eighteenth century and being murdered.

The barmaid, Miss Margaret Marshall, spending her first night there, suddenly found herself wide awake in the middle of the night. She said she was absolutely terrified. 'I couldn't hear or see anything but I felt the warmth of someone in the room. Everyone laughed next day but night after night I had the same awful feeling that someone was roaming round the room. I changed the furniture about, trying to get rid of the sensation, but it wouldn't go.'

Then the proprietor bought some old pictures and among them was one of a woman being murdered a century or more ago by a burglar who broke into the room occupied by Miss Marshall.

In 1970 a television engineer went up into the attic of the inn to erect an aerial. He hurriedly returned 'as white as a sheet' and refused to go up there again alone. He would not say what he had seen but there could be no doubt that something had really terrified him. The place where he had been working was directly above the 'haunted' bedroom.

According to Andrew Green the ghost was last reported seen in August 1972. It would be tempting to suggest that a female phantom seen here might be Lady Hamilton for documentary evidence exists in Torquay museum to prove that it was a rendezvous for her and Lord Nelson but the ghost, if ghost there is, seems to be an unidentified lady who was murdered in her bed.

Combe Martin

In the autumn of 1921 a lady artist visited the church of St Peter. As she quietly closed the door behind her she became aware of the screen door opening and she saw a bishop emerge, complete with mitre and crozier, dressed in a cream and gold gown and followed by six sturdy priests who carried a large tray containing a fawn-coloured wax model of a walled city, some four feet square. A procession of ladies, courtiers and peasants followed, their costumes, the artist thought, dating from about the fourteenth century. As she watched, thinking that she must be witnessing a re-enactment or pageant of a dedication ceremony, the artist suddenly realized that the whole event was taking place in complete silence and as she became aware of this fact, the entire procession, having walk-

St Peter's Church, Combe Martin: ' . . . a bishop emerged, complete with mitre and crozier, followed by six sturdy priests and a procession of ladies, courtiers and peasants.'▶

ed nearly the length of the aisle, faded away and completely vanish-ed.

According to *Devon and Cornwall Notes and Queries* for 1965-7, the ghost of Squire Usticke was seen by his housekeeper on the day of his funeral. She was in the sitting room, waiting for the return of the mourners, when she saw her dead master enter the room and sit down in his usual chair. Astonished, she went forward to greet him and found that he had disappeared and that the chair was empty. As she sat down again to compose herself the first of the mourners returned from the burial of Squire Usticke.

Dartington

Fourteenth-century Dartington Hall is justly famous for its deep in-volvement with the land and nature and for the great beauty and ut-ter peace of its gardens. Small wonder that the historic house, which, over the years, has seen almost every kind of intrigue and tragedy that can be imagined, is haunted. But it is no violent ghost that haunts these hallowed walls, not a victim of any tragedy, nor is it anything to do with the vicious jousting and cruel bear baiting that undoubtedly took place on the green terraces here.

Nor has it anything to do with the 'frolic' ladies who once lived here: either the one who married William Polglas within three days of the death of her father and married again within two days of her first husband's death; nor yet the Lady Roberta whose dark and doubtful deeds are not recorded but a Special Act of Parliament was passed to enable her husband to divorce her!

No, it is a gentle shade that blends with the quiet and dignified beauty of this house and grounds that you may be lucky enough to encounter, perhaps on the cobbled path beside the ancient kitchen or down the steps beside the Irish yew trees, known since time im-memorial as 'the twelve apostles'; there or anywhere in this haven of peace you may suddenly be aware of a white lady or some other figure from the long past, for such forms have been seen here: quiet, unalarming, congenial ghosts, completely at peace in this wonderful place, unable or unwilling to leave and who would blame them.

The white lady ghost, according to tradition, always appears before a death. In 1890 she was seen by a maid three weeks before

Richard Champernowne, the rector of Dartington, died; and again three weeks before another member of the family died in India in 1897.

The Countess' Room also has a ghost legend. The wife of Gawen Champernowne—the first Champernowne at Dartington Hall—was the daughter of the Count of Montgomerie and there is evidence to suggest that she was repeatedly ill-treated by her husband whose jealousy knew no bounds. Tradition has it that he eventually shut her up in this room where she died and her ghost now haunts the room, a pathetic, silent form that is sometimes glimpsed wringing her hands in despair.

There is too a ghostly old lady whose footsteps have reportedly been heard in the third nursery and there are stories of children waking to find an old nurse bending over their beds.

The drawing room has been the centre of a curious psychic echo for here exquisite music has been heard emanating from the locked

Dartington Hall: ' . . . you may suddenly be aware of a white lady or some other figure from the long past . . .'

and empty room. The etheric and indescribably beautiful music has been reported by witnesses outside the room; when the door is opened all is immediately quiet, but those who have heard this unearthly music have never forgotten it.

There is a persistent belief that a lady once threw herself off the old church tower here and that a tree marks the spot where she fell. Here a ghostly grey lady, or grey nun, has been seen. A visitor was driving by, not very long ago, when he chanced to exclaim to his passengers that there was something in the road ahead and he clearly saw a figure in grey that suddenly disappeared. Two of the three occupants in the car also saw the figure in the car's headlights before it completely and inexplicably disappeared.

Finally a ghostly headless horseman of unknown origin is said to emerge through the lowest gate in the drive near the river. Reports of headless horsemen have interested me for years and a radio programme on the subject, that I helped to compile and contributed to, is preserved in the archives of the BBC as being of historic interest.

Dartmoor

'There is something very mysterious in the eerie shapes of the vast masses of granite that form the many tors and the no less queer gigantic screes on their sides known locally as "clitters"'. So wrote S.P.B. Mais in 1928 and it is no less true today, particularly if the very strange stories of the 'hairy hands of Dartmoor' have any foundation in fact.

This story first came to the attention of the general public by means of an article in the *Daily Mail* of 14 October 1921. It was reported that at least three accidents had occurred in the summer of 1921 in exactly the same spot, Nine Mile Hill, on the road into Postbridge.

In March 1921 a doctor and two children were travelling along this road in a motorcycle with a sidecar when the doctor suddenly called out that something was wrong with the controls and he told

◀Near Postbridge on Dartmoor: ' . . . a pair of large hairy hands closed over his own and forced him off the road.'

**Dartmoor: 'There is something very mysterious
in the eerie shapes of the vast masses of granite . . .'**

the children to jump out, which they did. The motorcycle swerved, skidded, the engine came completely adrift from its fastenings, and the doctor was killed. The children survived. It later transpired that the motorcycle had recently been overhauled and no explanation was ever forthcoming as to the cause of the accident.

A few weeks later a coach swerved at exactly the same spot, for no apparent reason, mounted the grass verge and jerked to a stop, bruising and shaking up all of the occupants; one passenger sustaining serious injury. The driver said afterwards that he felt invisible hands pull the steering wheel out of his grasp.

On 26 August 1921 a young soldier was riding his motorcycle along this stretch of road when he hit the side and was injured; again at exactly the same place as the previous accidents had occurred. He said later that it seemed to him that a pair of large, muscular and hairy hands had closed over his own and forced him off the road.

In 1924 a lady was staying in a caravan at Powder Mill, near the haunted spot, and one night she saw a pair of hairy hands at the caravan window. She made the sign of the cross and prayed hard and nothing else happened but it was an experience she never forgot.

According to Ruth St Leger-Gordon there were manifestations of the mysterious hairy hands long before 1921. She recounts in her *Witchcraft and Folklore of Dartmoor* (1965) stories of pony traps overturning; cyclists feeling their handlebars suddenly wrenched out of control; horses that shied, bolted and threw their riders; cars and motorcycles skidding and crashing, sometimes with fatal results.

She tells too of an accident in 1961 when a young man was driving from Plymouth to Chagford one evening. He never arrived at his destination and was found dead underneath his car, near the same spot where other unexplained accidents have happened. Expert examination of both the man's body and the car failed to reveal any satisfactory explanation of the accident.

I once spent a night in my car near this 'haunted' place and although I rested undisturbed my dog, usually very adaptable and at ease as long as I am there, was restless all night, wandering round the car, growling and sometimes showing all the signs of terror. She evidently saw or felt something that was beyond my senses of perception.

Dartmouth

When I was at the Royal Castle Hotel some years ago I learned that on occasions visitors and staff have reported hearing unexplained sounds, most frequently in the autumn and usually about two o'clock in the morning, in the vicinity of a former doorway that led into the courtyard; a doorway that has been shut and altered for many years and now forms part of the hallway.

Mrs Gwyneth Powell had been manageress at this historic establishment for nearly twenty years and she told me she had never seen anything but she had heard the ghost sounds many times. The full range of the noises, according to various witnesses, begins with the sound of a galloping horseman; then there is the rattle and clatter of several horses pulling a coach over cobbles and into the courtyard; then there are heavy footsteps, the banging of coach doors, the shouting and whipping-up of a team of horses and finally the rumble and rattle of a departing coach.

Mrs Powell said the coach is always on time. On every single occasion she has heard the clock striking two o'clock, but of course the sounds do not occur every night or even with any regularity as far as has been established but she has heard them during the months of September, October and November but most frequently in October.

The ghostly coach is thought to have its origin in an historic episode concerning William and Mary. Princess Mary had crossed the Channel and was waiting for her husband at this quayside inn. A storm, and the possibility of an unenthusiastic reception, caused William and his army to change course and they put in at Torbay. News of the alteration in William's plans came to Mary by special courier, a messenger who rode by way of Totnes Bridge to tell her that a coach was on its way to take her, with all speed, to Brixham. It arrived shortly before two o'clock in the morning.

Where now the naval college stands on Boon Hill once stood the residence of Squire Boon and his beautiful daughter on whom he doted. Her choice for a husband settled on a young man who at first found favour in the eyes of her father but then he changed his mind; he decided the man was not good enough for his only daughter and he succeeded in extracting from her a promise that she would not marry him.

Soon the Squire died and sometime later, feeling perhaps that she was now released from her promise, the girl married her young man and they went to live at Mount Boon a few months after the wedding.

They had hardly settled in before strange happenings began to take place. Unearthly noises were heard, heavy furniture moved by itself and flames of light were seen that seemed to follow the couple about the house. Could her father reach her from the grave? They left the house on the hill and went to live in London but the ghostly manifestations seemed to follow them and before long they returned to Mount Boon. There, after a short respite, the ghostly activities

Royal Castle Hotel, Dartmouth: '. . . there is the clatter of several horses pulling a coach over cobbles . . .'▶

were resumed and by now the girl was convinced that her father's ghost was responsible.

The distracted couple called in the clergy and had the place exorcised but still the strange noises and disturbing happenings continued. Then, by some means that is not disclosed, the ghost seems to have made a bargain: he would return to the grave and haunt the house no more if his daughter would accompany him . . . she agreed, hoping to trick the ghost, who promptly disappeared; but oddly enough the girl died less than three months later. Local people believe that the ghost of Squire Boon still haunts the grounds, sometimes appearing on horseback and at other times on foot, seeking perhaps to put right the evil he did in pestering two young people whose only crime was to be in love.

Dunchideock near Exeter

Haldon House was built in 1735 with Buckingham Palace as its model. Parts have been demolished over the years, parts have been altered, but the property, once owned by Sir Robert Palk, Governor of Madras, has apparently been haunted for many years. One story tells of Sir Robert having two sons who continually quarrelled until eventually one 'disappeared' and it is his ghost, it is said, that is responsible for various nocturnal raps and taps and he is thought to be the male figure that has been seen flitting silently behind glass-panelled doors. Unfortunately, for the sake of authenticity, Lord Haldon—as Sir Robert Palk became—had only one son — so perhaps the identity of this particular ghost has not really been established.

Mr and Mrs Ron Martin, who once ran the property as a guest house, said that a number of their guests complained of being awakened between midnight and three o'clock in the morning by taps on their bedroom doors. The Martins were themselves disturbed by hearing a voice calling their Christian names but whenever they opened the door the corridors were deserted and all was quiet. They said this ghost only haunted one floor of the property. One guest, a hospital matron, thought she heard her name called and she became so distressed and frightened that she refused to leave her room at night for the rest of her stay.

Most of the many guests who reported seeing the figure of a man on the ground floor did not know they had seen a ghost. Usually only the head and shoulders were visible and they appeared to be quite normal; until it was shown to them that it would be quite impossible for a real person to be where the figure had been seen.

A later occupant stated that two of her guests told her they had heard the sound of horses' hooves and the snapping of twigs at dead of night and they said they had seen the figure of a servant girl.

The present house is in fact the original servants' quarters; the main part of the house became dangerous and was destroyed early this century.

**Haldon House: ' . . . a male figure has
been seen flitting silently behind
glass-panelled doors.'**

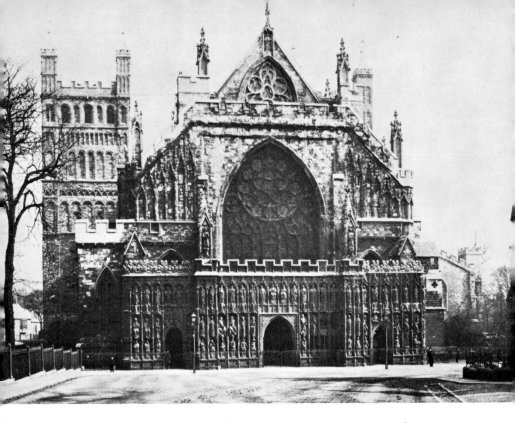

Exeter Cathedral: 'The ghost of a nun is reputed to
appear at seven in the evening in July.'

Exeter

The ghost of a nun is reputed to appear in the Cathedral at seven
o'clock in the evening during the month of July, emerging from the
south wall of the nave and disappearing through the south wall of
the Church House. Several houses in the Close, including the Dean-
ery, have long been reputed to be haunted.

A former Bishop of Crediton, the Right Reverend Wilfred
Westall, told Deryck Seymour in July 1961 that his house in the
Close was undoubtedly haunted. As soon as they moved in, he said,
his son had complained of disturbed nights caused by the sound of
heavy breathing beside him in his bed. Suggestions that it might be
the cat proved untrue. The door of this particular bedroom was
heard to open by itself many times when it had been most carefully

closed and it would be heard to close by itself whenever it was left open. A most contrary ghost! The Bishop added that the sound of deep breathing and the unexplained movement of the door had been heard and witnessed by many people. A present inhabitant of this house states that she once saw a monk standing beneath an archway in the house; the figure seemed to smile at her and then promptly vanished.

Nearby a house was occupied by the organist, Lionel Dakers, who maintained that he and his wife heard the sound of footsteps on the stairway and in the upstairs portion of the house. These sounds were always heard during the late evening and were quite inexplicable. At first the parents naturally supposed that the sounds must originate from one of their children and Mr Dakers went up to see that all was well, only to find the children sleeping peacefully. Other people, residents and visitors, have occasionally reported identical sounds in the property that was rebuilt after being bombed.

Other ghosts at Exeter include the spirit of Queen Henrietta Maria who is said to walk in the garden of Barnfield House, a frail-looking figure dressed in seventeenth century costume. It is known that this unhappy queen stayed in Exeter to have her baby in safety before fleeing to France. Then there are the mysterious ghost children at an hotel in the city which used to be an old house. They have been seen in the yard at night which is lit up as if it were daylight with the children running round and playing.

In the cellar of a shop next to the Guildhall the manager and other witnesses have heard the rustle of silk and seen a spectral figure resembling a woman with staring eyes. She is thought to be the victim of a crime committed in the dungeons which extend beneath the Guildhall, a crime that dates back more than two hundred years.

Exeter University has a modern ghost. The form of a decorator in white overalls has been seen from time to time walking silently through the corridors. He is thought to be a workman who returns to admire his handiwork!

Cowick Street has two ghosts. The Cowick Barton Inn occupies ground where there once stood a monastery and a ghost monk is seen periodically both within the precincts of the present inn and in the nearby fields. A newsagents' shop used to have a ghostly skeleton and a ghostly black boy that haunted the vicinity of a cupboard under the stairs. After the stairway was altered during renovations

both ghosts disappeared.

In September 1979 Miss Dorothy Warren, a member of The Ghost Club, spent several nights at an hotel close to St David's Station and one night she found herself suddenly wide awake at about 2.30 a.m. and she saw a shadowy form in her room . . . as she sat up in bed the form disappeared. A couple of nights later she again found herself awake in the early hours and this time there was a menacing male figure standing beside her bed with hands reaching for her throat! She had time to notice a round head with receding, dark, straight hair and a dull jowl; the figure had powerful shoulders and a thick body. He seemed to be dressed in the fashion of the 1750s with a white collarless shirt, slightly tucked around the neckband and fullish sleeves set into a ruff; he also wore a leather waistcoat and since he was so close to the bed she could not see below waist-level but she had the impression of breeches and stockings.

With commendable pluck Miss Warren addressed the apparition and told him, in no uncertain terms, to clear off. A surprised look came over the face of the form bending over her, and the next moment he had disappeared. Subsequently Miss Warren made a number of enquiries and concluded that the present hotel occupies the site of a much earlier building, probably an inn frequented by farmers, merchants and other dealers who may have made money on market days. Inns were often of doubtful integrity two centuries ago and few questions were asked about missing people or bodies found in the nearby River Exe. Miss Warren felt that her experiences at the hotel were probably some kind of psychic echo dating from an actual happening of long ago.

A correspondent tells me that when she lived in a house in Exeter it was undoubtedly haunted. She was taken there at the age of five, with her nanny, to live with her grandparents. They had a large house and while the front stairs were carpeted, the back stairs leading from the kitchens, were not.

Every year, towards the end of September, my informant would be awakened from sleep, late at night, by the sound of someone running up uncarpeted stairs and she used to call out, 'Nanny, don't run up the stairs; you wake me up.' She would get no reply but she

◀' . . . there was a menacing male figure standing beside her bed with hands reaching for her throat!'

would hear a door slam on the landing above. Even as a child she was puzzled by the fact that the footsteps, clearly on uncarpeted stairs, sounded from the front stairway that was carpeted.

Years later, after they had left the house, her grandmother told her the story of the running footsteps. The hall had one of those tiled floors and anyone downstairs would hear the footsteps run by. When she had first heard the footsteps the grandmother thought that it must be her daughter, who lived nearby; but of course the door was locked and the daughter was certainly not responsible for the sounds. She had become used to the unexplained footsteps and had told Nanny not to say anything about them to the child as she didn't want her to be frightened. She and others had often heard the heavy footsteps rushing up the front stairs, sounding as though they were on boards and she would then hear the sound of a door slamming on the landing above; but only in the month of September.

When my correspondent's grandfather was dying in the house, her grandmother moved into one of the bedrooms on the top landing at about the time of year when the footsteps were usually heard and, much later, she told her grand-daughter that she was never able to sleep comfortably in that particular room because, during the month of September, it would often suddenly become very hot and then as suddenly become very cold and these extreme changes of temperature would sometimes continue all night. She also said that as a young child herself she used to wake up and find a small boy crying, at the foot of her bed.

Years later she learned that other people who had slept in that room had also seen the little boy. They were unable to trace any history of violence in the house but they thought that the crying boy and the running footsteps must be connected in some way. The mystery was never solved and continued all the years they occupied the house.

Hartland

The Parish Church, situated at nearby Stoke, is dedicated to St Nectan and there are many people who believe that this Saint haunts the churchyard. St Nectan is credited with miraculously

View from Hartland Quay

picking up his head and replacing it after he had been decapitated in the early days of English Christianity.

This attractive Church is well worth a visit apart from its phantom monk. There is a handsome Norman doorway, a grotesquely carved Norman font, a fine cradle roof and a beautiful rood screen. Some ancient stocks and part of the old pulpit, inscribed to King James, are preserved in a little room over the porch.

A few years ago, in 1973 to be exact, when the Reverend Harold Lockyer was Vicar, he was convinced that he saw the ghost monk on two occasions. Once the figure of a monk appeared momentarily in the aisle of the church. The figure seemed to be 'a common or garden monk in a black habit' said Mr Lockyer. 'I was not deluded,' he added. 'Neither had I been drinking at the time.'

Another afternoon, while walking across the graveyard, he noticed a figure on the path leading to the Church, a figure that was approaching an old yew bush covering a large tombstone. 'The figure was a mere twenty feet from me at the time,' the vicar reported. 'I could see that it was the figure of a man in a brown monk's habit with his head bent forward and the hood well covering his features. I stood for a moment, waiting for him to approach. It was rather unusual to see a monk hereabouts and I wondered who it was. Then, as he walked towards me I walked towards the path to greet him and the next moment he simply vanished—just disappeared in front of my eyes.'

In August 1981 I asked Mr Lockyer about the experience and inquired whether, as far as he knew, the figure had been seen again. Mr Lockyer, now Vicar of Axminster, tells me that to the best of his knowledge the figure of St Nectan has not been seen again. 'But then,' he adds, 'as I have not been in Hartland, it would be unlikely for me to hear about it.' In fact I learn that members of the congregation and casual visitors to St Nectan's Church have sometimes noticed the figure of a monk, but the form has always been taken to be a normal person visiting the area. When the figure disappears in puzzling circumstances the observers wonder whether they have seen the phantom monk.

There are other ghosts at Hartland. The road running beside the

St Nectan's Church, Stoke: 'Once the figure of a monk appeared in the aisle of the church.'▶

Abbey is reputed to be haunted by a ghostly procession of monks. Near Bow Bridge there is a tradition of two headless lady ghosts, clad in silken dresses which can be seen and heard as the figures move. Incidentally, strange spectral lights have long been seen in the vicinity of Bow Bridge and one witness has described the lights as being about twenty inches in diameter, white in colour with ultra-marine centres, and quite stationary. They are usually seen at a height of twenty to thirty feet above ground level and they remain visible for upwards of a minute before suddenly vanishing.

Blind Road—a private road through Hartland Abbey to Black-pool Mill—is reputed to be haunted, occasionally, at midnight by a phantom man in white riding a phantom white horse. There is also a persistent belief that Docton Bridge is haunted by a ghost calf and for years no local person would willingly pass that way on winter nights.

Ilfracombe

The best-known haunting here is associated with fifteenth-century Chambercombe Manor House which I first visited more than thirty years ago. When the manor was sold I was sent a detailed prospectus of the property which was advertised as 'Manor House for sale—complete with ghost'.

One of the hauntings here seems to have been triggered by the discovery in 1865 of a secret room. The then owner was intrigued when he noticed a small bricked-up window where, as far as he knew, there was no room. After an interior wall had been broken down he was able to look into a low, dark, secret chamber and, as his eyes grew accustomed to the darkness, he beheld its sinister contents. He could make out in the dim light what appeared to be the remains of a perfectly furnished room. Amid the cobwebs and the dust of years he could see too the remains of rich tapestry still covering some of the walls. There was a chair, a table and a four-poster bed-stead with the curtains drawn. By the light of a flickering candle, hurriedly brought at his request, he made to draw back the curtains from the four-poster, but they fell to dust at his touch and as the bed itself was revealed he saw, lying on the bed, the skeleton of a young woman, a few remnants of her garments still covering the white bones. The remains were buried in a pauper's grave in Ilfracombe churchyard.

Inquiries suggest that the remains may have been those of Kate Oatway, daughter of William Oatway, a known wrecker who lived at Chambercombe in the seventeenth century and it has been surmised that he killed his own daughter when she threatened to expose him and his friends to the authorities. Another story has it that the remains are those of a titled lady who was taken to Chambercombe when the ship in which she was a passenger was wrecked near Hele beach, below the Manor. After she had been robbed and abused and was of no further use to her captors she was perhaps walled up in the little room and left to die. It is known a tunnel once ran from Chambercombe to Hele beach; a tunnel that was almost certainly used by smugglers and wreckers.

Whoever the pathetic victim may have been, whose remains were found in the secret room, her ghost is said to have walked after her

Chambercombe Manor: ' . . . he saw, lying on the bed, the skeleton of a young woman . . . '

often heard than seen, although on two occasions two female members of the family had seen her: once at dusk and once early on a summer morning.

It seems that ghostly footsteps have frequently been heard in upstairs bedrooms and sometimes there are accompanying sounds that suggest jewellery and trinkets are being handled and turned over. Once there was the sound of beads dropping to the floor and indeed so distinctive was this that the young lady hearing the sounds thought that her own necklace had broken and she looked down, expecting to see the beads on the floor. Nothing has ever been found that might account for the sounds and no story is known of previous occupants that suggest why the place should be haunted.

The Augustinian Priory has long had the reputation of being haunted by a phantom monk, a daylight ghost that is usually seen standing by one of the priory walls, although on one occasion the ghost reportedly moved close to the priory but kept pace with a horse and trap in which the witnesses were riding. Thirty years after this sighting a ghostly nun appeared during Mass in the chapel of the Priory and was witnessed by all the worshippers present, some of whom thought it was a vision of the Virgin Mary herself. However, from time to time, reports filter out of a ghost nun being seen in this chapel so it would appear that the place is haunted by a nun and a monk and one wonders what event or series of events sparked off these ghostly appearances and spectral wanderings and whether they are connected in any way.

A ghostly coach and horses used to haunt the area of Four Firs on the Buckfastleigh road, usually appearing between midnight and one o'clock; more recently the sound only of horses, a coach and mourners, has been reported from the same place at the same hour. Perhaps the haunting is fading as some hauntings do, the visual aspects being the first to go leaving the sound until eventually that too disappears, almost like a battery running down.

Lapford

The churchyard of St Thomas of Canterbury and the surrounding village is reputedly haunted by the ghost of a murdering Rector. In the 1800s a Curate attached to the Church was killed by the Rector who was duly charged with the murder but at the trial the Reverend John Arundel Radford was found 'not guilty' by the jury who reputedly stated : 'They had never hanged a parson yet and weren't going to start now.'

So the Rector continued his parochial duties here until his death in May 1867, but before he died he was aware that in view of what had happened there were likely to be difficulties in carrying out his wish to be buried in the chancel of the church, so he stated that if this was not done his ghost would return. This threat was ignored and the Rector lies buried in the churchyard where an inscription on a stone cross reads: 'In Memory of John Arundel Radford, Rector of this Parish' but the ghost of Radford has been seen many times in the churchyard, wandering among the gravestones, as though unable to leave . . . yet, if reports be true, his ghost has also been seen occasionally elsewhere in the village.

The village has another ghost, a much older recurring phantom, in the shape of St Thomas à Becket, murdered in Canterbury Cathedral on 29 December 1170. His form is supposed to ride through the village and past the church bearing his name each 27 December, on his way to meet Tracey, who lived nearby; a man who was to become known as one of the murderers of Becket.

Lewtrenchard

Lewtrenchard House was once the home of the Reverend Sabine Baring-Gould (1834-1924); in 1872 he inherited the estate where his family had been settled for nearly three centuries and he exchanged his living as Rector of East Mersea in Essex for that of Lew Trenchard in 1881.

He is the author of many books: fiction, folklore and mythology. His *Book of Were-wolves,* published in 1865, was much sought after until it was re-published in 1973, being described as 'the classic work on this dreadful subject'. His fascinating *Curious Myths of the Middle Ages,* (1866), is still a source book of considerable interest and value; but perhaps he is best known as the author of the famous hymn, *Onward Christian Soldiers.* He must have been an interesting man but it is the ghost of an eighteenth-century Madam Margaret Baring-Gould who once haunted the family home that concerns us here. Perhaps she still does for a little girl visitor apparently saw the ghost of a 'dear old lady in old-fashioned dress' in the 'haunted' gallery in 1967.

Madam Margaret Baring-Gould was a woman of strong character: she built up the family estate after the death of her husband in 1766 and she died sitting in a chair in 1795, having refused, point blank, to be put to bed. As she died all the window shutters of the house threw themselves wide open and a servant, entering a bedroom to close the shutters, looked out of the window and was astonished to see the figure of her mistress, who had died less than an hour earlier and whose corpse lay in the house, standing under a walnut tree, seemingly looking up at the servant.

If the ghost of Madam Margaret is bound to the house in some way which we do not understand, she does not appear to be confined, as are some ghosts, to the house and grounds for she has been seen in the surrounding countryside.

There is certainly a lot of evidence to suggest that one corridor or gallery, extending the whole length of the upper storey of the house, is particularly haunted. Here the White Lady—or Madam Baring-Gould—has long been said to walk at dead of night and 'her step', wrote Sabine Baring-Gould, 'has been frequently heard'. He says that his mother often told him how she had heard the steps at night, as though proceeding from high-heeled shoes, although at first she had thought it must be her husband coming to bed. Years later Baring-Gould himself heard the crunching of unseen carriage wheels on the drive and the peals of mocking laughter that greeted anyone who looked out to see who was arriving.

Madam Baring-Gould had been in her grave only a week when her ghost was seen, this time by a responsible man named Symonds. He saw her one evening in a field in the Lew Valley and there was nothing ghostly about the figure. Symonds had just returned to this country from America; he had known the redoubtable Madam Baring-Gould and had a considerable respect for her. He had no idea that she was dead and he waved to his friend who, he noticed with some surprise, seemed to be dressed in white satin with long shoulder-length hair blowing in the breeze. He smiled as she waved

' . . . and her step has been frequently heard', wrote Sabine Baring-Gould (right) of the White Lady. ▶

back at him and he noticed the distinctive diamond ring on her finger, sparkling in the moonlight.

In the years that followed, her ghost was seen many times: walking over Galford Down; standing by the Dew Pond; loitering in the lane beside an old mineshaft, where she once so frightened a witness who recognized her that he broke a leg in his hurry to get away; in the present drawing-room of Lewtrenchard House, sitting by the side of the fireplace where she often sat in life; in the 'haunted' gallery of course and also in some of the bedrooms, especially it seems if there is a sick child therein.

So frequent were appearances of the ghost more than three decades after Madam Baring-Gould's death in 1832 that a carpenter was employed to open up the vault in Lewtrenchard Church where the body of Madam had been buried beside her husband. As the tomb was opened it is said that the ghost of Madam Baring-Gould appeared and chased the frightened workman across the fields to his home!

When my friend James Turner visited Lewtrenchard House in 1972 he was delighted to learn from the owner that the ghost of Madam Baring-Gould had been seen within the previous five years. It seemed that a young man and his fiancée enjoyed many visits to Lew House when it was an hotel; they spent their honeymoon there and returned regularly for holidays. Their daughter Joanna was conceived there. In 1967, when the little girl was five years old, Joanna and her parents were staying at the hotel once more and during the night Joanna felt unwell. She got up and wandered along the gallery to a lavatory. Her parents, hearing her leave the bedroom, followed a moment later and heard her talking to someone in the gallery where a light was always left on at night. They could see nobody and when they asked their daughter who she had been talking to, she replied that 'a dear old lady in old-fashioned dress' had asked her whether she was unwell and what her name was. The child had felt no fear and had replied, 'I'm Joanna, who are you?' The old lady had answered, 'I'm Margaret, my dear', and then, as Joanna's parents approached, the gentle ghost of Madam Baring-Gould quietly disappeared.

**Lewtrenchard Church: 'As the tomb was opened . . .
the ghost of Madam Baring-Gould appeared . . .'▶**

Little Haldon

At the side of a quiet road here, between two farm properties,there is a ruined fourteenth century chapel that has long had the reputation of being haunted by the ghost of a mad monk.

Six centuries ago it is said that this monk was in the habit of luring passing travellers into his cell, on the pretext of hearing their confessions. As soon as the opportunity presented itself, the unfortunate traveller would be murdered or knocked unconscious; he would be robbed of such worldly goods as were on his person and then the body, dead or alive, would be thrown down a convenient and deep well.

A variation of the story has the monk escorting unwary visitors across Haldon Moor before dealing with them in a somewhat similar manner. One day he is said to have enticed a sailor into the little chapel but when he was about to deal with the stranger as he had dealt with so many people before, the sailor was quick, too quick for the rascally monk, and he was the stronger man. Within a few minutes it was the monk who was dead and whose body disappeared down the well.

The phantom head and shoulders of the murderous, mad monk have reportedly been seen hereabouts from time to time; usually at dusk and most frequently by lone travellers or passers-by. Several variations and enlarged versions of the story exist; one example will give an idea of the way in which it has caught the imagination of some interested people.

This story, also concerning a sailor, tells of a solitary man of the sea making his way home after some years voyaging round the world and carrying on his person many valuables and the not inconsiderable proceeds of his services. He is met by a friendly monk who persuades him to rest awhile in the roadside chapel. Soon the conversation turns to the sailor's spiritual welfare and the forgiveness of sins and before long the sailor humbly kneels to receive absolution. Hearing an odd sound behind him, he opens his eyes and turns to see the monk poised over him with an upraised dagger and murder in his eyes.

Eventually, in the desperate fight that follows, the sailor overcomes the monk who falls or is pushed down a well. Shocked and shaken, the sailor blurts out his story to the first person he encounters. Together they hurry back to the little chapel and the monk is hauled out of the well, more dead than alive; but in the well are found the remains of numerous human beings—previous visitors of the monk who were less fortunate or less strong than the sailor. Local legend does not tell us what eventually happened to this murdering fourteenth-century monk, if he did survive the battle with the sailor or whoever his last victim may have been; but it is claimed that his ghost still haunts the roadway, sometimes the complete form of a seemingly friendly monk that disappears when it is approached, but more often only the head and shoulders, the upper part of a man's bloated body that seems to ooze itself out of the ground, twisting and writhing and struggling, as though trying to extricate itself from a well that no longer exists. Strangers to the locality, with no knowledge of the story of the mad monk have reported hearing the sound of two men engaged in a desperate struggle, sounds that emanate from within the confines of the ruined chapel; and sounds that cease instantly when the puzzled visitor approaches the deserted building.

Haldon House, with its twenty-two bedrooms, used to be very haunted as I have already mentioned in the entry on Dunchideock. The hill down from Little Haldon towards Teignmouth also has the reputation of being haunted and in August 1978 Deryck Seymour tells me he had firsthand evidence of the haunting from a couple who were driving very slowly down the hill, since they did not know the area and they had plenty of time to spare. After a while, that still summer morning, they reached a junction where a lane joined the road from the left and here the driver became aware of a car approaching this junction and instead of giving way, this car came straight into the major road, causing Deryck Seymour's informant to brake violently to avoid a collision. The car that had caused this disturbing incident then proceeded towards Teignmouth and the couple, somewhat shaken, followed, but a few hundred yards along the road the car ahead of them suddenly swerved and turned right into what appeared to be the drive of a private house. Imagine their surprise when they drew level with the spot to find no turning of any kind, only a thick hedge. The mysterious and badly driven car was clearly seen by both the occupants of the following vehicle, when it came into the main road and when it disappeared from view. It may be significant that there are frequent skid marks in the area:

perhaps the disappearing car is seen by other road users who skid to avoid it.

Luffincott

Between Holsworthy and Launceston a few moss-covered stones mark the site of a once-famous haunted rectory. In 1838 the Reverend Franke Parker took the living—now combined with Clawton—and virtually rebuilt the existing rectory; adding a bow-window here and a conservatory there, stone-flagging the floor, thatching the roof and generally enlarging and beautifying the one-storey building in its idyllic setting. He lived there for forty-five years, a bachelor, a scholar of the black arts and an eccentric.

His books he guarded jealously and once left the pulpit in the middle of a sermon and hurried back to the rectory because, he said, his servants were looking at his books. A former policeman said the

The ruined coach-house at Luffincot Rectory

Rector would sometimes suddenly sit up in his chair and bark like a dog and some of his parishioners believed that he had the power to turn himself into a lion or a toad. He reportedly said in all seriousness, more than once: 'Bury me deep when I die, so that I might not rise again.'

After his death he was succeeded first by the Reverend T.W. Maurice and then by the Reverend S.C. Haines; neither stayed long in the well-endowed living with easy duties and an apparently charming rectory

In 1894 the Reverend T.W. Browne went to Luffincott; another bachelor, partly paralysed and described by the local people as 'a queer old chap'. Before long he was living at Clawton and walking to Luffincott to perform his clerical duties. The reason he left his own rectory? Because he believed he saw the ghost of Franke Parker. One sighting of the ghost was enough. He left the house at once, hurried to his old lodgings at Clawton and never lived at Luffincott rectory again, nor would he allow any of his possessions to be brought out of the house. On Sundays he would drive over with his landlord in a pony and trap, conduct the services and eat his lunch in the church porch.

Gradually his furniture and possessions were surreptitiously removed from the house and sold and, as the story of the haunted rectory that could not be lived in spread around the countryside, people interested in such matters visited the house and even spent nights there, hoping for some experience of the preternatural happenings; sadly we have no record of whether or not they encountered the ghost of Franke Parker or indeed any superphysical manifestation but a few years later, either by accident or design, the house was destroyed by fire and with it the unquiet ghost of Franke Parker seems to have disappeared.

Marldon

Parts of Compton Castle, a National Trust property, have long been reputed to be haunted. In more than one book devoted to haunted places it is stated that the dungeons have that doubtful honour but I am informed that Compton Castle has no dungeons!

Centuries ago the solar basements in early houses were sometimes made into a parlour and a fireplace supplied; at Compton the basement was heightened two feet as is evident from alterations to the solar fireplace so perhaps this is the area that has been described, erroneously, as the dungeons. Certainly I possess evidence of a ghostly figure, that seemingly dates from some three hundred years ago, being seen here.

Compton Castle is in fact a fortified manor house that was built in the fourteenth, fifteenth and sixteenth centuries; a house that was the home of Sir Humphrey Gilbert, half-brother of Sir Walter Raleigh, and it remained in this family until 1800. It is likely therefore that it is a ghost of the illustrious Gilbert family that haunts Compton, if ghost there is, for witnesses have described a figure in seventeenth century costume that has been encountered in various parts of the house but especially in the vicinity of the gabled tower; a figure that is seen but briefly, often at dusk on winter evenings; a shy ghost that disappears almost as soon as it is glimpsed, leaving the observer wondering whether it was just a shadow after all.

Moretonhampstead

I am indebted to Deryck Seymour for the information about two haunted houses in this village that has become known as the gateway to Dartmoor. He tells me that when he first visited Millbrook in 1952 it was no more than a deserted cottage, a few yards from the road and reached by means of a short, grassy lane. It was the last property in the village and although there were houses a short distance away, yet it had an air of remoteness in its sheltered hollow. In front of the house there was a maze of kitchen gardens, long since overgrown, stretching down to the stream a few yards below; the garden given over to pig-styes and poultry runs belonging to a local baker, Mr Underhill.

Previously the cottage had been occupied by the Milton family who left during the Second World War on account of the dilapidated condition of the property. During the war years Mr Underhill used to go to Millbrook to lock up his poultry and he did so one frosty winter's night when snow was a foot deep, arriving there about 9.15 p.m. It was bright moonlight and just beyond a hedge on the far side of the stream Mr Underhill saw a figure. As his lantern was not too well blacked-out, in accordance with war-time instructions, he wondered whether it might be the police and he called out, 'What's up then?' The figure made no answer but seemed to crouch down and then proceeded to move rapidly towards the stream where it suddenly vanished. Puzzled, Mr Underhill immediately followed and crossed over the stream. Not only was no one there but there was no disturbance in the snow: whatever he had seen had left no imprint behind. Next morning he was still mystified as to what he could have seen and why there were no tracks and he returned to the cottage as soon as he had the opportunity. There had been no fresh snow during the night and his own footprints were still clear but there were certainly no other marks of any kind.

On another evening Mr Underhill was once again tending his poultry, accompanied by a friend this time, when his companion was suddenly struck backwards by a force that they both distinctly heard come whizzing towards them. Something seemed to seize the unfortunate man's throat in a strong grip and he fell backwards, only to be released as quickly as he had been invisibly seized. Again the time was about 9.15 p.m.

This same friend of Mr Underhill was inside Millbrook one summer evening when he saw, through the open door, a fair-haired boy, clad in a blue sweater and grey socks, running along the garden path. 'Where are you going, son?' he called out. 'That path is a dead end . . .' As he spoke he stepped through the open doorway and was thoroughly bewildered to find no sign of the boy! The child he had seen so plainly seconds before had completely disappeared. As the boy had had his back to the cottage the man figured that he should have heard his footsteps as he approached but looking back on the incident he realized that he had heard no sound whatever. As he stood in the garden, puzzled and bewildered, the church clock struck 9.15 p.m.

On yet another occasion when he was at the cottage, Mr Underhill placed a bucket of water in the middle of the path for a moment. When he was a few yards away he heard it overturn and found that the rim of the bucket had been pushed down so hard into the earth that it was necessary for him to give it a hefty tug to get it clear. Again it was around 9.15 p.m. and it was at the same time on another evening when Mr Underhill's dog suddenly stopped in the middle of the path and started to whine, its coat bristling with fear. Mr Underhill could see nothing and it was a clear night but there was no persuading the dog to move, either backwards or forwards, until eventually it became calmer and made its way to the road, its tail between its legs. Mr Underhill joined my friend Deryck Seymour on a ghost watch at Millbrook and they were particularly vigilant when the time was around 9.15 p.m. but that night neither watcher saw nor sensed anything unusual.

An old house in Ford Street, now demolished, had a back bedroom that terrified most people who ever attempted to sleep there. When Mrs Radcliffe lived in the house, her daughter used to wake up 'scared stiff'. Often she would find herself awake in the middle of the night and hear heavy, shuffling footsteps. When she slept in the room on one occasion Mrs Radcliffe heard the shuffling footsteps herself and saw a pair of eyes staring at her from the darkness. Later the sound of heavy furniture being moved could be heard when the room was unoccupied. Enquiry established that the room had once been occupied by a young girl who had an unhappy love affair and she had committed suicide in the room.

Northam

A few years ago, soon after the Morwenna Park council estate was completed, many people who lived in the vicinity of 'Humpty Dumpty Hill' complained that they had seen strange ghostly forms in their houses; that crockery and ornaments had mysteriously shattered; that furniture had inexplicably broken and that household appliances were constantly going wrong. In fact many of the people who moved here said they had had nothing but bad luck ever since the houses were built and they appealed to the local Vicar for help.

The Reverend Michael Lewis visited some of the houses and blessed them to exorcise the 'bad luck' and although there did not appear to be any immediate improvement, after a while things did gradually seem to get better.

One of the worried women, Mrs Mary Braithwaite, said at the time: 'Things began to go wrong as soon as we moved in. I started

Okehampton Castle is 'reputedly haunted by the ghost of "the wicked Lady Howard" . . .▶

76

Percy, who was thirty-one; three years later he was dead. Next she eloped and married Thomas, son of Lord Darcy but within a few months Thomas was dead. She then married Sir Charles Howard and bore him two daughters before he too died. Her fourth and last husband was Sir Richard Grenville, a 'tiresome and quarrelsome fellow' who also predeceased the tireless Mary.

The keeper of Okehampton Castle will sometimes exhibit the ballad that tells the story of the ghost of Lady Howard and the Coach of Bones and he may tell you about the time his deputy saw the ghostly Lady Howard, sitting, combing her hair . . .

Plymouth

TSW Studios were built, I have been told, on the site of an old cemetery where French sailors were buried who were washed ashore during the Napoleonic Wars. A few years ago a nightwatchman was informed, when he first took up his duties, that one part of the studios—one of the largest sets—was haunted. Subsequently he and others, who were unaware of the reputation of that particular set, reported hearing on more than one occasion, 'a hard and cruel laugh' when they were alone in the deserted studios. At the same time the atmosphere was found to have become suddenly very cold. A thorough search and check of the entire building revealed no sign of anything to account for the experiences.

Princetown

The grim prison here was built in 1806 to house French prisoners of the Napoleonic wars and then adapted for use as a convict station in 1850. The old burial ground has long been reputed to harbour several ghosts, reportedly seen from time to time by both prisoners and warders.

◀TSW Studios, Plymouth: . . . 'a hard cruel laugh' was heard in the deserted studios.

Perhaps the best known ghost of The Moor is old David Davies, a prisoner who first went there in 1879 and who was to spend fifty years in Dartmoor Prison, much of it tending a herd of sheep. He became known as the Dartmoor Shepherd and at lambing time he was so trusted that he was allowed to spend nights on the moor tending the expectant ewes.

There is a story that at the time of his eventual release he asked to be allowed to remain at the prison and when this request was refused he asked for his shepherd's job to be kept open for him, saying, 'I'll be back'. He was back in prison within a few weeks and eventually died there in 1929.

After his death there were a number of reports of his familiar figure being seen shepherding the sheep through the swirling mists that so often shroud the precincts of the old prison. And even today there are occasional sightings of the elusive and indistinct form of Davies disappearing from sight almost as soon as he is glimpsed in the areas he knew so well during his long sojourn in this lonely place.

In 1963 a visitor, Mrs Greenaway, was staying at the Prince of Wales Hotel and found herself wide awake on three successive nights at 3.30 a.m., awakened by the sound of a ghostly alarm clock, although subsequent enquiries elicited the fact that no such clock was to be found on the premises.

On the second occasion she also saw what she described as a small white triangle floating downwards in her dark bedroom. The third time she found herself awake she also heard the sounds of soft music being played. These events and experiences were judged to be of sufficient interest to be included in the *Transactions of the Devonshire Association* for 1964.

Sampford Peverell

This little place acquired considerable notoriety in 1810 and for years afterwards through activities that became known as the 'Sampford Ghost'. The Reverend Caleb Colton, who had personal experience of the disturbances, recounted the full story in his *Narrative of the Sampford Ghost*, published at Tiverton in 1810.

The affected house was occupied by the family and servants of Mr

Dartmoor Prison: ' . . . his familiar figure . . .
shepherding sheep through the swirling mists . . .'

John Chave and long before the arrival of the classic poltergeist activity there were stories of the house being haunted by the ghost of a woman, allegedly seen by an earlier occupant who had also reported unexplained noises and other disturbances.

The better-known ghostly manifestations began in April, 1810, when the 'chambers of the house were filled, even in daytime, with thunderous noises and upon any persons stamping several times on the floors of the upstairs rooms, they would find themselves imitated—only much louder—by the mysterious agency!' There were a number of women servants and at night they were reportedly beaten by invisible hands until they were black and blue; this happened many times. Mr Colton stated that he heard upwards of two hundred violent blows in one night delivered upon a bed, the sound resembling that of a strong man striking it with all his might, with clenched fists. One of the young servant girls, Ann Mills, received a black eye and a swelling as big as a turkey's egg on her cheek. Ann was among those who received blows from an invisible hand while in bed. Mrs Mary Dennis and young Mary Woodbury, two other servants, swore that they were beaten until they were numb and were sore for many days afterwards.

The disturbances became so bad that the servants refused to use the room in which they were so severely handled whereupon Mr and Mrs Chave offered to share their own room. Still there was little peace, well-attested disturbances taking place nightly: candles and candlesticks were only two of the items that moved about the room of their own volition. Once Mr Chave narrowly missed being hit on the head when a large iron candlestick came hurtling at him in the dark. Colton relates how he 'often heard the curtains of the bed violently agitated, accompanied by a loud and almost indescribable motion of the rings. These curtains, four in number, were, to prevent their motion, often tied up, each in one large knot. Every curtain of that bed was agitated, and the knots thrown and whirled about with such rapidity that it would have been unpleasant to be within the sphere of their action. This lasted about two minutes and concluded with a noise resembling the tearing of linen, Mr Taylor and Mr Chave, of Mere, being also witnesses. Upon examination a rent was

◀' . . . narrowly missed being hit on the head when a large iron candlestick came hurtling at him . . .'

found across the grains of a strong new cotton curtain.'

Raps, knockings, rattling noises and a 'sound like that of a man's foot in a slipper coming downstairs and passing through a wall' were repeatedly experienced. Once, says Mr Colton, he was in the act of opening a door when there was a violent rapping on the opposite side. He paused and the rapping continued: suddenly he opened the door and peered out, candle in hand. There was nothing to see. Sometimes the noises were so violent in a room that he really thought that the walls and ceiling would collapse.

Among the independent witnesses of the Sampford ghost is the Governor of the County Gaol, who came to see the strange happenings and brought with him a sword, which he placed at the foot of the bed, with a huge folio Bible on top of it. Both were flung through the air and dashed against the opposite wall, seven feet away. Mr Taylor, who was in the house at the time but not with the Gaol Governor, was roused by the shrieks coming from the room and when he entered he saw the sword, suspended in the air, pointing towards him. Within a moment it clattered to the floor.

Towards the end of the curious events at Sampford Peverell there were suggestions that the tenant, Mr John Chave, was faking the disturbances in order to purchase the property cheaply. When this rumour reached the people of the village and those of Tiverton, five miles away, public sympathy for the occupants of the house quickly melted away and on more than one occasion Mr Chave was very severely handled. The Reverend Caleb Colton rejected this explanation, stating that although the public were given to understand that the disturbances had ceased, in fact, as the immediate neighbourhood well knew, they continued 'with unabating influence'. Mr Chave had no intention of buying the property, said Mr Colton; indeed, he was making every effort to procure another home, on any terms. As if to confirm all this, the disturbances at length obliged the whole family to leave the house, at great loss and inconvenience. Mr Colton was criticized for his participation in the affair. It was not generally known that he offered £100 of the total of £250 to be paid to anyone who could give such information as might lead to a discovery of the answer to the mysterious events; the money was never claimed.

Years later it was discovered that the house had double walls, with a passage between, which could have considerably assisted conscious trickery. There was also the possibility that the premises were used by smugglers who might have produced the weird noises for their own purpose—and, of course, many a parson was known to help the smugglers in days gone by.

Shute

Shute House used to be Shute School and shared the grounds with Shute Barton, the ivy-clad gatehouse and surviving wing of the old Tudor mansion of the de la Pole family. Here there is a Grey Lady ghost who enjoys parading along 'The Lady Walk', a path bordering the playing field.

A few years ago, during the course of a school Sports Day, several of the parents present mentioned to the school staff that they were somewhat puzzled by the 'rather strange woman' in grey who seemed to glide rather than walk along the edge of the sports field, a woman who seemed to be totally unaware of the proceedings and who 'walked up and down as though she owned the place' but who 'blandly refused to answer their questions'.

The staff, somewhat bashfully, had to admit that their phantom 'Grey Lady' had probably put in one of her periodical appearances as she had been in the habit of doing, on and off, for as long as anyone could remember.

Shute Barton once belonged to Lady Jane Gray's father; it was a Royalist stronghold during the Civil War and the original 'Grey Lady' is thought to have been a certain Lady de la Pole who was hanged for her Royalist sympathies. Indeed the story goes that she was hanged from a tree on the estate, a tree that withered and died and disappeared, unlike the ghost of Lady de la Pole which is still seen occasionally, sometimes through a window and almost invariably in the area known as 'The Lady Walk'.

Stowford

The ghost page boy of Hayne House is one of the stories collected by the late Lord Halifax and included in his fascinating *Ghost Book*. It seems that in 1885, when Lord Halifax was staying with his father-in-law at Powderham Castle, among the guests was a Lady

Ferguson Davie, who one evening related the story that has since been retold and re-written countless times. For this account I have gone back to the original.

About a century ago now Mr Harris of Hayne House was robbed and he lost a good deal of his valuable family plate. At the same time a little page boy, who had been in his employ for a while, also disappeared. Every effort was made to trace both the boy and the plate but to no avail and Mr Harris was so upset by the whole affair that he eventually shut up the house and went away for a long holiday.

One night, shortly after his return, he thought he saw the missing page boy standing at the foot of his bed and supposing that he must be dreaming, or that his imagination was playing some trick, he turned over and went back to sleep. Next night the same thing happened. Again he found himself awake in the middle of the night and again he thought he saw the little page boy standing beside his bed. But again Mr Harris took no notice and returned to sleep.

The following night he awoke yet again to see the figure of the page boy in his room and this time he got up out of bed and, when the figure of the boy turned and left the room, he followed. The boy led him along a passage, down the stairs and across the hall, always keeping a little way ahead of him but constantly turning round, as though to make sure that his master was following.

At length they passed out of the house and Mr Harris was led to a small wood close by and here the boy disappeared, at the foot of a very large and hollow tree.

Next day Mr Harris had the tree cut down and inside were found the remains of the missing page boy and some of the stolen plate. The discovery caused a considerable stir and apprehension among the staff and eventually a confession on the part of the butler to the effect that he had made away with the plate little by little as opportunity occurred and that he had hidden it in the hollow tree until he was able to dispose of it. The page boy had discovered what was going on and the butler and his wife had killed the boy and concealed his body in the tree with the plate.

To this day a stone is pointed out as marking the place where the

◀Shute: ' . . . the strange woman in grey seemed to glide rather than walk . . . '

butler murdered the page boy and buried the body and apart from the occasional reported re-appearance of the ghostly page boy inside the house, his ghost also haunts the nearby road, and there are other ghosts at Hayle House according to the *Transactions of the Devonshire Association Report on Folklore* for 1964.

There is a ghostly black dog — one of many in Devon — that haunts the grounds in and around Hayne Park; there is a headless man, some say he carries his head under one arm, that haunts the terrace and is supposed to always appear when any master of the house dies; there is a little old lady ghost in the King Charles Room; and ghostly knocks are said to be heard from time to time in one of the old rooms.

Tavistock

When my friend James Turner was writing his *Ghosts in the South West* published in 1973 I went with him to visit historic Kilworthy House, a mansion built by the formidable Elizabethan, Judge John Glanville, whose rich and ornate tomb can be seen in Tavistock Church, the nose of his effigy missing, struck off in the Civil War. He must have been a strong-minded man of considerable determination for it fell to his lot to condemn to death his own daughter, Elizabeth, for the murder of her husband. Perhaps it is not surprising that such a powerful personality should have persisted beyond the grave.

In 1833 the wife of the then Vicar of Tavistock, writing to Robert Southey, says it was common knowledge in the town that the Judge 'walked' the grounds and the ruins of his former home. Today the ghost of Judge Glanville is still said to haunt the terraces he built and to appear quite frequently on the Judge's Seat, below the massive yew trees that he planted.

Sadly the Elizabethan house that Glanville built fell upon evil times. That edifice has all but disappeared among the considerable alterations that took place in the reigns of Charles II and George III. The front was entirely rebuilt, and it is unlikely that externally Glanville would recognize his mansion although some of the interior remains much as it was in his day.

James and I were welcomed to Kilworthy House by Steve

Cawdray, an American and headmaster of the tuition centre for maladjusted children that the house had become. The property had been given to a Charitable Trust by the owner and Principal, the Reverend John Lyon, Vicar of Bickleigh. And this Vicar was among many people who asserted that they had encountered the ghost of the Judge's unhappy daughter, Elizabeth, who, although in love with a local young man, had been forced by her father to marry another, an old miser named Page who paid the Judge handsomely for his daughter's hand.

Elizabeth still saw her lover, George Sandwich, and when he learned of the harsh and cruel life she was forced to live, he decided — or perhaps he was persuaded for both Elizabeth and her maid were also involved — to put an end to Page. One night neighbours were awakened by a rumpus in the Page house at Plymouth and a young man was seen at the window. A snatch of conversation was heard, suggesting that some evil deed had been committed. The fol-

Kilworthy House: Judge Glanville, who condemned his own daughter to death, 'walks' the grounds.

lowing morning old Page was found dead and hurriedly buried. On the testimony of the neighbours however the body was exhumed and suspicious marks were found on the neck suggesting that the old miser had been strangled. Elizabeth, Sandwich and the maid were all tried and executed. Judge Glanville, Elizabeth's father, pronouncing the sentence.

At Kilworthy House I have seen a door leading from the courtyard into the Great Hall, part of the original Elizabethan house, that often opens by itself and closes of its own accord, with a loud slam. Many times it has been carefully closed and even jammed shut, but still it opens by itself and closes with considerable noise; and still the ghost of the tormented Elizabeth haunts the house her father built.

In 1965 a plumber, working in the house, saw her at the top of the main staircase; three years later, the then matron of the school felt an unmistakable presence at the same spot, the top of the main staircase, and heard the swish of a floor-length dress. About the same time the Reverend John Lyon's sister saw and felt the same apparition or manifestation and was so surprised and astonished that she found herself unable to move a muscle.

One Saturday in June, 1971, the Reverend John Lyon saw the ghost girl himself. He was in bed, reading, late at night and waiting for the return of some students who had been granted late passes and he knew they would look in on him when they returned to say goodnight. Suddenly through the open door he saw the ghost of Elizabeth Glanville. She was slim and on the short side. She wore a dark cloak and hood which perhaps accounts for the fact that the face was not visible.

Although I have received no reports that the unquiet ghost of Elizabeth Glanville has been seen or heard recently I feel the atmosphere at Kilworthy House is conducive to ghosts and I would never be surprised if this well-documented ghost from the first Elizabethan age were to be encountered again at any time.

Tiverton

The remains of the castle are reputedly haunted by a sad ghost, a girl who had just been married and killed herself accidentally.

Tiverton Castle is thought to have been built by Richard de Redvers, first Earl of Devon, in the reign of Henry I, and dismantled after the Civil War. Parts of the fourteenth century structure still stand — the banqueting hall, a tower, the chapel and a gateway — and these are the parts that are said to be haunted; other portions of the original castle have been altered and turned into private residences.

The Courtenays once lived at Tiverton Castle and it may be a ghost of this famous family that haunts the place where perhaps she knew some brief happiness. The story has a parallel with the tale of the Mistletoe Bough Chest associated with Bramshill and Marwell Hall and several other places in Hampshire.

It is said that the young lady of the family had been married only a few hours before she met her death. Legend has it that a large carved chest, part of the castle furniture, was discovered by the bride as she took part in a game of hide-and-seek enjoyed by the younger guests immediately following the wedding ceremony.

As her friends sped through the castle seeking somewhere original to hide, the young bride ran off alone and coming across the carved chest in a shadowy corner of one of the corridors, she hastily climbed inside before anyone could see her and, as she heard footsteps approaching, she quickly lowered the lid. There was an ominous 'click' as a spring lock snapped into place and to her horror the terrified girl discovered that she could not open the chest from inside and furthermore so stoutly made and well-fitting was the chest that it was virtually soundproof. In the hot darkness of the prison in which she had confined herself, the distraught girl soon expired.

The hours passed and the games came to an end but where was the lovely young bride? Guests and family searched high and low, calling her name and seeking her in every room but they all overlooked the dark chest in the shadows. In any case it seemed to be locked so how could she hide inside.

Much later when the chest was eventually opened the yellowing wedding dress covered little more than a skeleton of the beautiful bride who had innocently hidden herself there. But over the years there have been occasional reports of the figure of a sad young bride wandering silently and sorrowfully through parts of the old castle, a figure that is glimpsed at the far end of a room or passing through a doorway or looking out of an ancient window; often by people who have no knowledge of the story or of the fact that the castle is haunted.

Other ghosts at Tiverton include the unexplained sound of a motor car that is sometimes heard during the months of December, January and February at Worth Lodge; and a hotel where a figure, believed to be connected with Richard Doddridge Blackmore, author of *Lorna Doone,* a man who may be said to have done for Devonshire what Scott did for the Highlands. It is surely appropriate that his ghost should walk somewhere in Devon.

Torbryan

The Church House Inn at this village near Newton Abbot has been reportedly haunted through several successive tenancies. Mick Heap took over in 1966 and before long he was encountering strange happenings; small and insignificant in themselves but viewed in the context of what the previous occupants had experienced, puzzling to say the least.

There was the time when Mick was locking up one night and he saw the cat suddenly show signs of intense fear: its hackles rose and it arched its back, staring fixedly at something in the corner of the room that was invisible to Mick. As soon as it could the cat seized the opportunity and dashed out of the bar and upstairs 'like a rocket', never before having been upstairs. It certainly seemed that it was determined to get away from something — anywhere. After that evening the pub dog would station itself on the landing of the stairs each night at the same time and bark and bark . . . nothing was ever discovered to account for the behaviour of these animals.

Before he moved in Mick had been told by his predecessor that he had been troubled by odd noises, footsteps clumping along the landing late at night and the occasional glimpse of a shrouded figure. Once, when the landlord's mother and father were looking after the pub while he went to a New Year's party, they were awakened around midnight by the door at the bottom of the stairs creaking as

Church House Inn, Torbryan: 'The ghost is generally thought to be a phantom monk . . .'▶

it opened and the sound of heavy footsteps on the stairs. As the foot-steps passed their bedroom, they called out: 'Happy New Year . . . you're home early, it couldn't have been much of a party.' They thought no more about the matter until they were awakened again just after five o'clock when their son really did arrive home! This is the staircase and the landing where a visiting Canadian said she felt an unmistakable presence one night and subsequently she refused to walk there alone.

The ghost form or figure is generally thought to be a phantom monk and such a form has been seen several times, once in the bar by a Royal Air Force officer who spent a night in the room and, by the light of the dying ashes of the fire, he saw what appeared to be a monk sitting on a chair at the other end of the room. As the officer, hardly able to believe his own eyes, quietly rose and approached the figure, it slowly melted away.

A village policeman who was new to the area called at the Church House Inn one day, during the course of making himself known to the local people and as he chatted to the landlord in the bar he idly asked: 'Who's the old man sitting over there by the wall?' There was nobody there but the policeman always swore that he saw someone who was there one minute and gone the next.

The Church House Inn was originally no more than a cottage, probably providing shelter and lodgings for the masons and monks building the nearby church and it is perhaps the shade of one of these early monks that is still occasionally seen, sitting in his accustomed place in the bar, enjoying the atmosphere of this peaceful and old and interesting pub.

Torquay

In Torquay there is a submerged forest and at rare intervals severe storms expose the stumps of trees, and remains of the same forest have been traced inland. The area has been described as 'thick with a primeval force' and many are the stories of strange and seemingly inexplicable happenings along this stretch of coast, both ashore and at sea.

Torre Abbey, founded in 1196 and once an important monastery, passed into private ownership at the Dissolution of the Monasteries. Among the earlier remains are a fourteenth century gateway, the entrance to the chapter-house, the refectory, and a barn known as 'the Spanish Barn' since the crew of an Armada galleon were confined there: all are reputed to be haunted. My friend Deryck Seymour is working on a history of Torre Abbey which is eagerly awaited.

Mr Lee, the Custodian of the Abbey in 1968, told Deryck Seymour that both he and his wife sometimes heard footsteps in the gallery of the Abbey. On each occasion a careful check was made and it seems that no human being could have been responsible for the sounds. Often too Mr Lee would feel, very strongly, that he was not alone when he was at work in his office and a visiting 'expert' once told him that there was a very evil influence there and that a murder had been committed thereabouts long ago.

Mr Lee was seeing Deryck Seymour out by the door at the top of the stairs in the Abbot's Tower, and my friend had just chanced to remark that it was a pity they could not go back in time and see something of the Abbey's past, adding that if it were possible he would choose to see the night when a mob broke into the precincts in the fourteenth century during the de Cotelforde trouble. Suddenly both men saw the latch being lifted and the heavy door swung violently open, right in their faces — and then as suddenly and inexplicably it slammed itself shut. This happened at ten o'clock on a bright summer evening and it was quite impossible for anyone to have come up the stairs and then got away without being seen, for the two puzzled men immediately searched the stairs and surrounding area very thoroughly. There was no wind, and in any case wind could not have lifted a latch; perhaps someone or something was annoyed at what Deryck Seymour had said only a moment before the curious manifestation!

The so-called Spanish Barn and the surrounding park is reputedly haunted by the figure of a young Spanish girl; a figure that presumably has haunted the place for nearly four hundred years. It is thought that no less than 397 prisoners were crammed into the barn after the capture of the Armada ship and disease and death soon wiped out most of them but at least one still walks where all her dreams and desires came to nought.

Before the Great Armada sailed from Spain the story goes that a young nobleman in the King's Army fell in love with a pretty Spanish girl and in their warm and romantic country the love affair

prospered and blossomed and the future seemed rosy until the Spanish Fleet was ready to sail. Then the young Marquis was assigned to the ship *Nuestra Senora del Rosario* and in youthful agony the lovers realized that they would soon have to part; or could they find a way to remain together? They talked it over and eventually decided on a desperate plan. The girl would dress as a page and so be able to accompany her lover on his voyage.

The whole of Spain was confident of a quick and easy victory over the lazy English and the young couple dreamed of the time when they would settle in some looted English manor house, given to the Marquis for the services he would render to his country, and there the lovers would live happily ever after.

But it was not to be. The Armada was defeated, the *Nuestra Senora del Rosario* was captured and the whole crew, including the Marquis and his 'page' were thrown into the ancient barn. There, in appalling conditions, the young Spanish girl was almost the first to die and the only consolation she was allowed, if we are to believe the story that has been handed down over the years, is that she received the last rites from a priest of her own religion who lived in the Abbey nearby. But even so she could not rest, it seems, and her form has often been seen, drifting sadly through the park on Torquay seafront, in the direction of the Spanish Barn, where she was with her beloved for the last few agonising hours of her life.

Prosaic motorists, driving along The Kings Drive late at night, are said to have seen her, especially when there is a moon; and since there are no reports of her lover joining her, perhaps it is only her shade that lingers in the area where she died and her spirit has been reunited with that of her lover in another sphere.

There is good evidence to support the story that the ghost of Henry Ditton-Newman, who died in 1883, played the organ at his own funeral — and occasionally returns to manifest himself inside the Church of St John's, where he was seen on several occasions soon after his death and at the 'haunted' Vicarage of St John's Church; an alternative theory is that the ghost of a man who committed suicide in 1953 is responsible for the later reported disturbances.

◀ The Spanish Barn: ' . . . she could not rest and her form has been seen drifting sadly through the park . . .'

From several sources I have heard that the church is haunted by the figure of the organist and by that of a previous Rector, Hitchcock, and there is no doubt that a number of parishioners and visitors claim to have seen the latter's unmistakable figure standing near the organ. Other people have said that they have heard the organ playing by itself and the music is thought to be the piece that Hitchcock was writing when death overtook him.

A former Vicar put on record the occasions when he heard the sound of organ playing and looked up to see his former and deceased organist seated at the instrument. The same organ — later replaced — used to be heard playing when no one was in the church, by the Vicar and others, sometimes at dead of night.

Montpellier House, formerly a choir school and adjoining the church, was much used by Henry Ditton-Newman; it is a house that was once haunted and may still be: unexplained footsteps were reportedly heard by several local clergymen and various visitors. The phantom form of Henry himself was reportedly often seen in a room on the top floor where there was 'a very strange atmosphere'; here there are many stories of disembodied footsteps and articles moving by themselves. The Reverend Sir Patrick Ferguson-Davie, Bart., once chased the footsteps, thinking he was about to catch a burglar, until they ceased at a blank wall at the bottom of the staircase.

Torquay also once had a very haunted house with a frightening ghost. 'Castel a Mare' in Middle Warberry Road stood derelict for years owing to its unsavoury reputation; everyone knew it was haunted. From Beverley Nichols I learned the full story of the remarkable experience he had there with his brother and Lord St Audries, a story he touched on in his autobiographical *Twenty-Five*.

It was a Sunday evening, after evensong, that the three young men found themselves outside the fearful-looking and dilapidated empty house, a house that for so long had been said to be haunted by strange sounds, screams and footsteps, following a murder there in the long distant past. Deciding to look over the house, they picked their way through the overgrown garden and entered through a window on the ground floor. They had a candle and went

◀' . . . he looked up to see his former and deceased organist seated at the instrument.'

101

from room to room; each seemed more melancholy than the last. The plaster had fallen in great lumps from the ceiling, boxes and planks were scattered all over the place, wallpaper hung in strips from the rotting walls. They found themselves talking in whispers as they climbed up the narrow twisting staircase to the upper floor.

At this stage Beverley Nichols went ahead and stood waiting for his companions in the upper hall. He told me that he was not feeling at all 'creepy'; rather disappointed, in fact, that nothing really frightening had happened, when he suddenly realized that his mind was working very slowly: his thoughts seemed to be reduced to a frightening slow motion. Then he became aware that the same thing was happening to his body. He felt as though a black film began to cover the left side of his brain and he remembered the time he had been anaesthetized. Just before everything was about to go black, he managed to stagger to the window, half-fall outside and then he lost consciousness.

He awakened to find himself sitting on the grass, feeling quite normal but strangely tired. He wanted no more to do with the house but his companions, who had experienced nothing strange in the place at all, were determined to return. Having established that Beverley was well again, they clambered back into the dark and silent house. After some twenty-five minutes spent in a very thorough examination of every corner of the property, including the little room from which Beverley felt the harmful 'influence' had emanated, they returned to him with the conviction that there was nothing whatever to be afraid of — the house was indisputably empty.

After a while Lord St Audries announced that he was set on exploring the house alone; he felt that Beverley's brother might be a kind of 'anti-influence' keeping the ghosts off, recalling that Beverley's experience had taken place when he had been alone. So, despite the objections of his friends, he went back into the house, after agreeing to take a candle with him and to whistle every few minutes, in reply to *their* whistles, to show that he was all right.

Beverley Nichols and his brother heard their friend clamber into the house, heard his footsteps cross the plaster-covered floor of the hall and heard him climbing the stairs. They heard him walk across the upper hall and then there was silence. They presumed that he had sat down as he said he would. After a moment they whistled and his whistle came back in reply, or seemed to, for the answering whistle seemed surprisingly faint. They whistled again and a faint echo came back. This went on for some twenty minutes, the answering whistles from the direction of the house seemingly getting stronger; then both Beverley and his brother sensed that 'something' came out of the house and past them, making no sound in the almost unearthly silence. Nothing was visible — when suddenly they heard Lord St Audries' voice: a cry, heart-rending and full of anguish; the sort of cry, Beverley Nichols told me, a man would make who had been stabbed in the back. He and his brother scrambled to their feet and rushed to the window. The sounds of a tremendous struggle came from upstairs: the wildest thuds and screams, as though a terrific fight was taking place. They didn't know whether to be frightened or relieved when at length heavy footsteps staggered down the stairs and Lord St Audries, a white-faced figure, his hair, clothes and hands covered with plaster and dust, emerged into the garden.

After a little while he was able to relate how he had found his attention being brought back time and time again to the little room Beverley had felt to be malevolent. He had sat with his eyes fixed in that direction. After a while he noticed a patch of greyish light in the darkness of the corridor; it was the door of the little room. He heard his friends' whistles and answered them for twenty minutes. Then, deciding that he had drawn a blank, he got up to return to his friends. At that moment, out of the room he had been watching, something came rushing at him, something that was black and seemed roughly the shape of a man although he could distinguish no face and the thing made no sound whatever. He found himself knocked flat on his back and a sickening and overwhelming sense of evil, as though he were struggling with something from hell, pervaded his brain. He fought as he had never fought before, forcing himself to his feet and then inching himself slowly down the stairs, thinking every second that he could go on no longer. At last he reached the bottom of the stairs and blackness but he was free from his adversary. He staggered outside and met his friends coming to his help.

Later the friends discovered that the murder in the house had been a double: a semi-insane doctor murdering first his wife and then a maid. The scene of the murders was the bathroom, the little room at the end of the corridor which had worried Beverley and Lord St Audries so much. The house stood next to one called

'Asheldon' in Middle Warberry Road, Beverley Nichols tells me, but the site has since been built upon.

Deryck Seymour, who lives in Torquay, tells me that he always found Upton Parish Church very interesting, from a psychic point of view. Back in September 1952, when he was organist at the church, he had parked his car outside the west door on one occasion while he went inside to collect some books that needed repairing. He was followed into the church by the late Herbert Sutton, another organist whom he knew well. The two men chatted for a while and then Sutton left while Deryck Seymour went into the vestry to collect some books. He then followed his friend out of the door. As he was leaving the church a little old lady in a maroon-coloured coat and black hat entered. She had snow-white hair and a pleasant, wrinkled face. She half-smiled at the organist as he stood on one side to allow her to enter. He took the books to his car, arranged them on the back seat, which must have taken all of five seconds, then went back for more books. By this time the old lady could have taken a few paces inside and possibly seated herself in a pew. Imagine

Weare Gifford: Sir Walter is still said to walk between the gatehouse and the church searching for his wife.

Deryck Seymour's surprise to find no one in the church. There were no other doors that were unlocked and realizing at once that he may have had a psychic experience, he ran out to find his friend, Sutton, who was only just getting into his car a few yards away. He then learned that Sutton too had clearly seen the little old lady and described her and her clothing exactly as Deryck Seymour had seen the figure. Sutton was quite prepared to swear that she was inside the church for had he not seen her enter himself and he knew there was no other exit and certainly she had not left by the west door as he could not have failed to see her. Both men searched the church from end to end but they found no trace of the figure they had seen, in daylight, in fact in bright sunshine.

Two vestries are built one above the other in this church and there is no ceiling to the floor between the two so that all sounds in the upper vestry echo clearly below. Deryck Seymour tells me he was often alone in the lower vestry of an evening, sorting music or something of the sort, and on several occasions he heard what he thought was the sound of footsteps entering the upper vestry but always on investigation he could find no cause for the sounds.

Weare Gifford

The picturesque Torridge sweeps round the ivy-clad and turreted old hall with its two contrasting ghosts. One is that of Sir Walter Gifford who died in 1243 and has walked ever since, between the fine gatehouse and the church, searching for his wife, it is said; the other is a lout of a ghost, a remnant ot some long-forgotten argument perhaps, the ghost of a common man of five centuries or more ago, who has been heard to murmur 'Get you gone . . .'

The church itself is haunted by the ghost of Sir Walter when he reaches it, a tall phantom who vanishes inside the hallowed walls. One cannot help wondering why Sir Walter Gifford is seeking his wife so earnestly and for so many centuries and what vivid and frantic incident in their lives can have caused this episode to be preserved upon the atmosphere of this charming place.

One legend says he walks at midnight looking for the wife he left; but why did he leave her, why does he walk at midnight, and why look for her in the church? There are those who assert that the old

The ghost at the Old Inn is known as 'Harry'.

knocker on the south door of the church resounds and echoes from his ghostly hand before his form disappears inside the church — only to reappear and re-enact the same scene upon some other midnight.

Widecombe-in-the-Moor

The church has its own legend of the Devil being responsible for knocking over one of the pinnacles during a visit he made to the village in 1638. In fact the damage was caused by lightning. Opposite the church stands the Old Inn where Uncle Tom Cobleigh and his pals enjoyed a few pints before they set out to become as famous as the fair that is held here each September — but that is another story; 'when the wind whistles cold on the moor of a night, all along, down along, out along lee; and Tom Pearce's old mare doth appear ghostly white . . .'

One ghost at the Old Inn is known as 'Harry' and he has been seen by many people, usually in the middle of the afternoon, walking from the kitchen into an adjoining room from which there is no other exit. He is often taken to be a real man for he appears to be quite solid and entirely normal, except that he disappears without explanation; 'just fades away' say those who have seen him.

The other ghostly happening at this fourteenth century inn is the sound of a crying child that has been heard in one of the upstairs bedrooms. Landlord, Geoffrey Ellis, heard the crying many times: 'it seems to last most of the night sometimes' but on investigation the room is always empty and silent until the door is closed again. A former landlord's wife said she heard it and checked time and time again: 'fitful, heartrending sobs, they are'. And Mrs Ellis is among those who have seen the ghost called 'Harry'.

The stories behind the sobbing child and the fading man, or perhaps the one story behind both ghostly manifestations, have been lost over the years but there is no doubt of the occasional reappearance of these aural and visual phenomena.

Nearby, about two miles north, near the House Tor Inn, there is an old grave with a worn headstone known as 'Jay's Grave', a grave that has long been the subject of speculation and puzzlement, for a bunch of fresh wild flowers are often to be found lying on the grave

Jay's Grave: ' . . . a dark figure has been
seen in the vicinity . . . '

and where they come from no one has discovered.

Mary Jay was a poor country girl who committed suicide after her
lover deserted her, leaving her to bear his child. She was buried here
in unhallowed ground where she hanged herself, according to the
custom of over a hundred years ago. In spite of periodical investigation nobody has discovered who places the flowers on the grave
although from time to time a dark figure has been seen in the
vicinity; a figure that disappears mysteriously. In 1967 a girl and
her boyfriend saw something dark crouching over the grave late one
night and, as they passed, the figure straightened itself up and
disappeared. The figure did not appear to have any legs and they
saw no face.

Select bibliography

Alexander, Marc, *Haunted Inns*, Frederick Muller, 1973,
Haunted Castles, Frederick Muller, 1974, *Phantom Britain*,
Frederick Muller, 1975, *Haunted Churches and Abbeys of
Britain*, Arthur Barker, 1978.

Brown, Raymond Lamont, *A Casebook of Military Mystery*,
Patrick Stevens, 1974.

Coxe, Antony D. Hippisley, *Haunted Britain*, Hutchinson, 1973.

Christian, Roy, *Ghosts and Legends*, David and Charles, 1972.

Green, Andrew, *Our Haunted Kingdom*, Wolfe, 1973, *Phantom
Ladies*, Bailey Brothers and Swinfen, 1977, *Ghosts of Today*,
Kaye and Ward, 1980.

Halifax, Lord, *Ghost Book*, Geoffrey Bles, 1939.

Hallam, Jack, *The Ghosts' Who's Who*, David and Charles, 1977,
The Haunted Inns of England, Wolfe, 1972.

Hole, Christina, *Haunted England*, Batsford, 1940.

Harris, John, *The Ghost Hunter's Road Book*, Frederick Muller,
1968.

Jones, Sally, *Legends of Devon*, Bossiney Books, 1981.

Legg, Collier and Perrott, *Ghosts of Dorset, Devon and Somerset*,
Dorset Pub. Co., 1974.

Loveridge, F.L. and E.A., *Devon*, Penguin (revised edition), 1954.

MacGregor, Alasdair Alpin, *The Ghost Book*, Robert Hale, 1955,
Phantom Footsteps, Robert Hale, 1959.

Mais, S.P.B., *Glorious Devon*, Great Western Railway Co., 1929.

Maple, Eric, *The Realm of Ghosts*, Robert Hale, 1964,
Supernatural England, Robert Hale, 1977.

Pearson, Margaret M., *Bright Tapestry*, Harrap, 1956.

St. Leger-Gordon, Ruth, *The Witchcraft and Folklore of Dartmoor*, Robert Hale, 1965.

Turner, James, *Ghosts in the South West*, David and Charles, 1973.

Underwood, Peter, *Gazetteer of British Ghosts*, Souvenir Press, 1971, *Dictionary of the Supernatural*, Harrap, 1978.

My Devon, Bossiney Books, 1981.

Shades and Spectres, Devon Folklore Register, 1978.

Wood, Margaret, *The English Mediaeval House*, Dent, 1965.

Acknowledgments

The author wishes to record his deep appreciation to everyone who helped him in the compilation of this volume and he feels that in particular he must mention Brian G. Birkmyre; Denise Marie Curran; D. Evans and the Mirror Group of Newspapers; Dr Peter Hilton-Rowe; The Revd Harold Lockyer; Beverly Nichols; H.J. 'Jim' Oliver and West of England Newspapers; Tom Perrott; Chief Officer A. Randle and J. May of H.M. Prison, Dartmoor; Deryck Seymour; Catherine Turner; Lt. Cdr. Nicholas M. Walker; Dorothy Warren; John Wildman; his publisher Michael Williams and, as always, his wife Joyce Elizabeth.

Peter Underwood

Further titles from Bossiney Books
available through your local bookseller

Ancient Dartmoor
Paul White

Dartmoor is covered with prehistoric settlements, stone rows and stone circles. Here is a simple introduction to current archaeological thinking, together with suggestions for which sites to visit. Full colour throughout.

Dowsing in Devon and Cornwall
Alan Neal

The art of dowsing is something Alan Neal, a professional dowser for many years, believes all of us possess. With the right tools, a little practice and maybe a map, you can locate anything you wish – lost keys, archaeological features, geopathic stress, ley lines and even spirits. This simple 'how to' book, which includes some of the author's favourite sites, also explains how you can date buildings, work out how much water is flowing underground and heal ailments... your limit is merely your imagination.

Ghost Hunting South-west
Michael Williams

Observations on the nature of supernatural phenomena – why they can be so elusive and yet at other times create such a dramatic impact. Drawing on case files from the West Country, some very recent, here are astonishing accounts of hauntings and people's reactions to their encounter with the unknown.

Mystery Cats of Devon and Cornwall
Chris Moiser

The popular press delights in 'The beast of Exmoor' and 'The beast of Bodmin', but what is the truth behind these sightings of big cats in the South-west? Chris Moiser, a biologist and local expert, draws from documented reports and investigations to provide some startling answers to this perplexing question.

Psychic phenomena of the West
Michael Williams

What is a ghost? Are animals psychic? How do people communicate with spirits? How can karmic astrology help? What do our dreams tell us? Do dowsing and spiritual healing really work? Michael Williams provides fascinating answers to some of life's imponderable questions.

Shortish Walks on Dartmoor
Paul White

Fifteen circular Dartmoor walks, typically 6-8 km (4-5 miles) in length. All have been selected for their beauty and their interest – enjoy finding prehistoric villages and ceremonial sites, medieval deserted villages and the massive diggings of former tin mines.

Spiritual Guides in the West Country
Jane E White

Many people are drawn to the West Country by its powerful charisma, which inspires a search into the universe's deepest mysteries. Here are the stories of a few spiritual seekers whose different paths in life reveal remarkable insights into mediumship, healing, numerology, past life research, psychic drawing, dream interpretation, guardianship of a sacred site, and spiritual teaching and painting.

Supernatural Dartmoor
Michael Williams

Granite tors and sweeping moorland, wide skies and wooded valleys – you cannot go far in this great stone-scattered landscape without encountering the strange and the inexplicable. Here are reports and personal accounts of paranormal activity in and around Dartmoor by a leading Ghost Club Society member.

UFOs over Devon
Jonathan Downes

The author saw his first UFO in 1997, and was astonished to find many other people had had similar experiences at the same time. Since then he has been researching UFO sightings, and discovered that UFO activity has been occurring in Devon for many decades.